Family Law
2012–2013

Routledge
Taylor & Francis Group
LONDON AND NEW YORK

Seventh edition published 2012
by Routledge
2 Park Square, Milton Park, Abingdon, Oxon OX14 4RN

Simultaneously published in the USA and Canada
by Routledge
711 Third Avenue, New York, NY 10017

Routledge is an imprint of the Taylor & Francis Group, an informa business

First edition published by Cavendish Publishing Limited 1997
Sixth edition published by Routledge 2010

British Library Cataloguing in Publication Data
A catalogue record for this book is available from the British Library

ISBN: 978-0-415-68339-5 (pbk)
ISBN: 978-0-203-30059-6 (ebk)

Typeset in Rotis
by RefineCatch Limited, Bungay, Suffolk

MIX
Paper from responsible sources
FSC® C004839

Printed and bound in Great Britain by
TJ International Ltd, Padstow, Cornwall

Contents

Table of Cases

Table of Statutes

Table of Statutory Instruments

Table of European Legislation

Conventions and Treaties

How to use this book

Welcome to this new edition of Routledge Tort Lawcards. In response to student feedback, we've added some new features to these new editions to give you all the support and preparation you need in order to face your law exams with confidence.

Inside this book you will find:

- NEW tables of cases and statutes for ease of reference

Table of Cases

Aluminium Industrie Vaasen v Romalpa Aluminium Ltd [1976] 1 WLR 676	14, 15
Andrews v Hopkinson [1956] 3 All ER 422	138
Armour v Thyssen [1990] 3 All ER 481	13
Armstrong v Jackson [1917] 2 KB 822	115
Ashington Piggeries v Hill [1971] 1 All ER 847	53
Barber v NWS Bank [1996] 1 All ER 906	37
Barrow Lane and Ballard v Phillips [1929] 1 KB 574	18, 19
Bartlett v Sidney Marcus [1965] 2 All ER 753	56
Bence Graphics International Ltd v Fasson UK [1998] QB 87	103, 184
Bentinck v Cromwell Engineering [1971] 1 QB 324	172, 173
Bowmakers v Barnett Instruments [1945] KB 65	171, 172
Branwhite v Worcester Works Finance [1969] 1 AC 552	140
Bunge Corporation v Tradax [1981] 2 All ER 513	120
Butterworth v Kingsway Motors [1954] 1 WLR 1286	37
Car and Universal Finance v Caldwell [1965] 1 QB 31	27
Central Newbury Car Auctions v Unity Finance [1957] 1 QB 371	25
Charge Card Services Ltd, Re [1988] 3 All ER 702	92
Clegg v Ole Andersson [2003] 1 All ER 721	66
Clough Mill v Martin [1985] 1 WLR 111	16
Colley v Overseas Exporters [1921] 3 KB 302	121
Couturier v Hastie (1856) 5 HL Cas 673	18
Cundy v Lindsay (1878) 3 App Cas 459	27
Demby Hamilton Ltd v Barden [1949] 1 All ER 435	11
Dimond v Lovell [2000] 2 All ER 897	153
Director General of Fair Trading v First National Bank [2001] 1 All ER 97	83, 185

Table of Statutes

Companies Act 1985	
s 395	14
Companies Act 2006	
s 860	14
Consumer Credit Act 1956	112
Consumer Credit Act 1974	2, 30, 31, 84, 112, 128, 130, 144, 145, 147, 150, 151, 154, 156, 168
s 8	129, 153
s 9(1)	129
s 11	134
s 12	134
s 15	131
s 17	134
s 19	135
s 33	173
s 34	173
s 39	145
s 39A	145
s 40	145
s 46	147
s 48	145
s 49	147
s 49(1)	145
ss 50–1	147

Revision Checklist

We've summarised the key topics you will need to know for your law exams and broken them down into a handy revision checklist. Check them out at the beginning of each chapter, then after you have the chapter down, revisit the checklist and tick each topic off as you gain knowledge and confidence.

1

Sources of law

- **Primary legislation: Acts of Parliament**
- **Secondary legislation**
- **Case law**
- **System of precedent**
- **Common law**
- **Equity**
- **EU law**
- **Human Rights Act 1998**

Key Cases

We've identified the key cases that are most likely to come up in exams. To help you to ensure that you can cite cases with ease, we've included a brief account of the case and judgment for a quick aide-memoire.

HENDY LENNOX v GRAHAME PUTTICK [1984]

Basic facts

Diesel engines were supplied, subject to a *Romalpa* clause, then fitted to generators. Each engine had a serial number. When the buyer became insolvent the seller sought to recover one engine. The Receiver argued that the process of fitting the engine to the generator passed property to the buyer. The court disagreed and allowed the seller to recover the still identifiable engine despite the fact that some hours of work would be required to disconnect it.

Relevance

If the property remains identifiable and is not irredeemably changed by the manufacturing process a *Romalpa* clause may be viable.

Companion Website

At the end of each chapter you will be prompted to visit the Routledge Lawcards companion website where you can test your understanding online with specially prepared multiple-choice questions, as well as revise the key terms with our online glossary.

You should now be confident that you would be able to tick all of the boxes on the checklist at the beginning of this chapter. To check your knowledge of Sources of law why not visit the companion website and take the Multiple Choice Question test. Check your understanding of the terms and vocabulary used in this chapter with the flashcard glossary.

Exam Practice

Once you've acquired the basic knowledge, you'll want to put it to the test. The Routledge Questions and Answers provides examples of the kinds of questions that you will face in your exams, together with suggested answer plans and a fully-worked model answer. We've included one example free at the end of this book to help you put your technique and understanding into practice.

QUESTION 1

What are the main sources of law today?

Answer plan

This is, apparently, a very straightforward question, but the temptation is to ignore the European Community (EU) as a source of law and to over-emphasise custom as a source. The following structure does not make these mistakes:

- in the contemporary situation, it would not be improper to start with the EU as a source of UK law;
- then attention should be moved on to domestic sources of law: statute and common law;
- the increased use of delegated legislation should be emphasised;
- custom should be referred to, but its extremely limited operation must be emphasised.

ANSWER

European law

Since the UK joined the European Economic Community (EEC), now the EU, it has progressively but effectively passed the power to create laws which are operative in this country to the wider European institutions. The UK is now subject to Community law, not just as a direct consequence of the various treaties of accession passed by the UK Parliament, but increasingly, it is subject to the secondary legislation generated by the various institutions of the EU.

1

Nullity

MARRIAGE AND COHABITATION

Definition of marriage

In *Hyde v Hyde and Woodmansee* [1866] marriage is defined as 'the voluntary union for life of one man and one woman to the exclusion of all others'.

Thorpe LJ in *Bellinger v Bellinger* [2001] suggested that marriage should be defined as 'a contract for which the parties elect but which is regulated by the state, both in its formation and in its termination by divorce, because it affects status upon which depend a variety of entitlements, benefits and obligations'.

Marriage is a legal agreement which creates certain rights and duties. These include:

- a duty to maintain under the Domestic Proceedings and Magistrates' Courts Act 1978 and under the Matrimonial Causes Act 1973, s 27;
- home ownership rights – on divorce the courts have the power to transfer the matrimonial home or a share of it to either party regardless of property law principles;
- duty to accommodate – right of occupation under the Family Law Act 1996 under s 30.

Cohabitation

Is not a relationship recognised in law like marriage and as a result cohabitees may not have the same rights on the break up of the relationship.

Marriage and Civil Partnership	Cohabitation
Married couples and civil partners have mutual maintenance obligations and courts have power to make maintenance orders.	There is no legal obligation to provide financial support for each other.
On termination of marriage court has the power under statute to adjust the parties' property and finance arrangements under the Matrimonial Causes Act 1973. This might include: ■ maintenance ■ financial provision ■ property adjustment ■ pension sharing	No statutory rights of occupation exist on separation. Cohabitees must use general rules of property law. ■ The principles governing constructive trust apply which are based on the 'intentions' of the parties. Either party might fabricate evidence making it difficult to prove.

On divorce indirect contributions will be taken into account.	■ The courts do not look at the future needs and resources of the parties. See commentary in *Stack v Dowden*[2007] ■ Under tight property laws the courts require a direct financial contribution to the purchase price. Claims for indirect contributions fail.
Both married parties automatically have parental responsibility for their natural child.	Only the mother has automatic parental responsibility. The cohabitee father may acquire parental responsibility: ■ by being registered on the birth certificate; ■ by agreement with the mother; ■ by obtaining a court order under s 8 Children Act 1989.
On the death of an intestate spouse the rules of intestacy apply, ie the remaining spouse has the right to succeed to his/her partner's estate on death.	Cohabiting couples have no right to succeed to their partner's estate in the absence of a will to that effect. A claim for reasonable financial provision may be possible under Inheritance (Provision for Family and Dependants) Act 1975.
Parties to the marriage have statutory rights to occupy the home under s 30 Family Law Act 1996 which are: ■ if in occupation, a right not to be evicted (s 30(2)(a)) ■ if not in occupation, a right to enter and occupy (s 30(2)(b)).	Cohabitee has no statutory rights to occupy the family home.
Various exemptions from tax apply to married couples and civil partners for example inheritance and capital gains tax. Fiscal policy varies according to Government.	Cohabiting couples are treated as two separate individuals for tax purposes and do not receive any special exemptions.

Couples that cohabit may face problems when their relationship breaks down. The law of equity and trusts may need to be used to enable either party to establish a beneficial interest in the home they occupied together. The legal mechanism used to establish a beneficial interest in a property is an implied constructive trust. The party must establish that there was a common intent to share the interest in the property. The question usually asked is 'is there any agreement, arrangement or understanding reached between the parties that the property is to be shared beneficially?' *Lloyds Bank v Rosset* [1991].

A common intent can be inferred from a direct contribution to the purchase price or mortgage instalment. The leading case on this area of law is *Stack v Dowden* [2007]. In addition to establishing a common intention the party must also establish that there was a 'detrimental reliance.' A detrimental reliance can be acts which show the party has relied on that common intention to his or her detriment. For example assuming joint liability for mortgage repayments. Although recent evidence suggests the need to establish this is diminishing.

Calculating the fair share that a party may be entitled to is not necessarily straight-forward. The question often asked is 'What would be a fair share for each party having regard to the whole course of dealings between them in relation to the property?' The Court should try and infer the parties' intentions from the surrounding circumstances. Although in *Stack v Dowden* [2007] it was highlighted that contributions do not necessarily need to be equal. The question to be asked according to Hale in *Stack* is not simply 'what is the extent of the parties' beneficial interests BUT did the parties intend their beneficial interests to be different from their legal interests and if they did, in what way and to what extent?' The burden will therefore be on the person seeking to show that the parties did intend their beneficial interests to be different from their legal interests, and in what way.

Reform

There is much discussion about how the law provides for cohabiting couples when a relationship comes to an end. Trust law is used to determine who is entitled to what property at the end of the relationship and many argue this can promote uncertainty and unfairness between the parties. This is reflected in the Law Commissions Report; *Cohabitation: The Financial Consequences of Relationship Breakdown* published in July 2007. Since its publication Lord Lester of Herne Hill presented the Cohabitation Bill 2009 in the House of Lords, which sought to determine specific rights for cohabiting couples on relationship breakdown and was largely based on the recommendations proposed by the Law Commission. The Bill was unable to complete its passage through the House of Lords due to a lack of time and as a result remains unimplemented.

The Bill aimed to provide basic protection in the event of a cohabiting couple:

- ceasing to live together; or
- the death of one of them; or
- enabling the life of either of them to be insured.

References to cohabitants in a relationship were to any two people (whether of the same sex or the opposite sex) who:

- live together as a couple; and
- meet the first and second conditions specified which are:
  - cohabitant couple are mother, father or parent of the same child
  - a joint residence order is in force in respect of a minor child
  - the cohabitants have lived together continuously for two years or more
  - are neither married to each other nor in a civil partnership of each other.

Although fewer than 1 per cent of marriages are now terminated by nullity petitions today, students still require a knowledge of this area.

The law of nullity encompasses non-marriages, void and voidable marriages. Each area has its own concepts and grounds for its existence.

NON-MARRIAGE

The ceremony which the parties undertook was of no legal consequence. The court therefore has no power to redistribute property and the couple will be treated as unmarried (*Gereis v Yagoub* [1997] 1 FLR 854; *J v C* [2006] EWCA Civ 551).

VOID MARRIAGES

There are social and public policy reasons as to why the marriage should not exist, as illustrated by the grounds contained in s 11 of the Matrimonial Causes Act (MCA) 1973. Due to public policy considerations, void marriages are void *ab initio.* This means in the eyes of the law that the marriage never exisited. The decree granted is declaratory but necessary to gain financial provisions. Also, third parties can challenge the validity of the marriage. There are no special defences.

Marriages celebrated after 31 July 1971 will be void on the following grounds.

Section 11(a)(i)

The parties to the marriage are within the prohibited degrees of relationship: either blood relations (consanguinity) or non-blood relations (affinity). See the

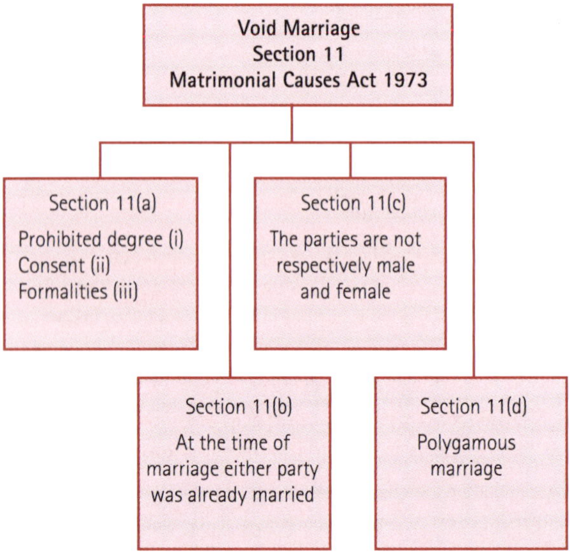

Marriage (Prohibited Degrees of Relationship) Act 1986. The bar preventing parents-in-law from marrying children-in-law was lifted following the case of *B v UK* [2005]. This case upheld the fact that preventing a man from marrying his daughter-in-law was a violation of the couple's right to marry under Article 12 of the European Convention of Human Rights. As a result the Marriage Act 1949 (Remedial Order) 2007 was passed removing this bar.

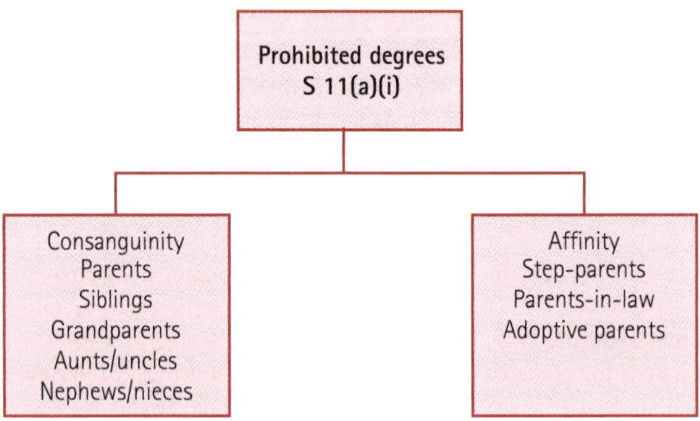

Section 11(a)(ii)

Either party is under the age of 16. However, if both parties are domiciled abroad at the time of the marriage, the marriage will be recognised as valid if it is recognised as valid in the country in which it was celebrated.

If either party is aged over 16 but under 18, then written consent is required from each parent with parental responsibility:

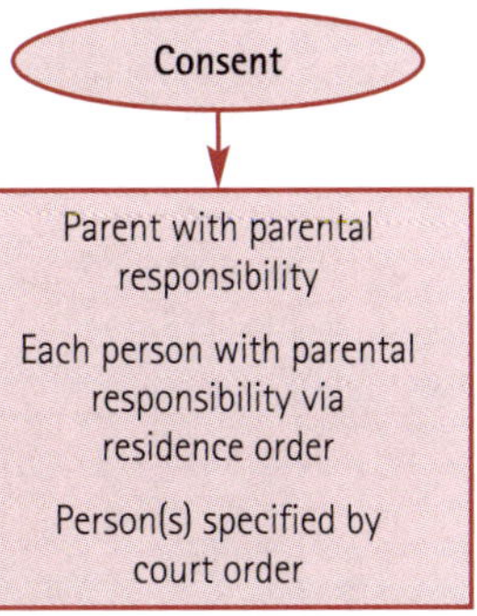

However, if this consent is lacking, the marriage will not be void unless the parents have publicly objected to the banns, thereby voiding them. An application can also be made to the High Court, county court or magistrates' court to obtain consent if the parents cannot give consent due to absence or inaccessibility.

Section 11(a)(iii)

The parties have intermarried in disregard of certain requirements as to the formation of marriage.

Publicity has been deemed necessary to prevent clandestine marriages, as illustrated by the existing rules, which are complex and are dealt with here only in outline.

Formalities for weddings

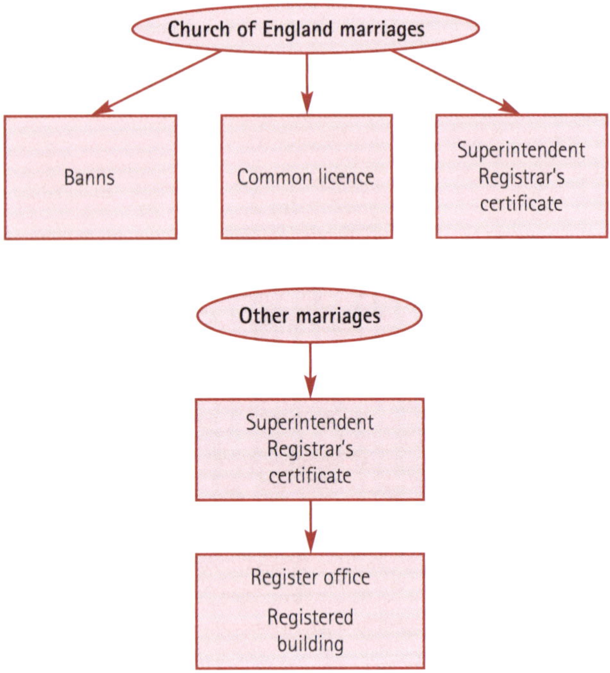

When there are defects in the formalities, the marriage will only be void if it is brought about 'knowingly and wilfully' by both parties (see box below) (*Gereis v Yagoub* [1997] 1 FLR 854).

◗ GEREIS v YAGOUB [1997] 1 FLR 854

The couple went through a purported marriage at a Greek Orthodox Church without going through legal formalities. The couple did not then follow up the ceremony by going through the legal formalities. They regarded themselves as married by only having sex after the ceremony, living together, and claiming

married couple's tax allowance. On breakdown of the relationship the Judge had to decide whether this was a void marriage or non-marriage. If the latter was the case the Judge would be unable to make any orders distributing the property.

The Judge decided that this was a void marriage as the couple had knowingly and wilfully married in disregard of the legal formalities under the Marriage Act 1949 rather than a scenario where the couple had pretended to marry as part of a charade.

Void

- No certificate/licence
- No banns/notice
- Banns not published properly
- Public objection to banns
- Over three months since banns
- Celebrant not qualified
- Building not approved/referred to in licence

Lack of consent: not necessarily void

Section 11(b)

At the time of the marriage, either party was already lawfully married.

This sub-section requires the parties to satisfy the definition of marriage contained in *Hyde v Hyde* [1866], that is, 'the voluntary union for life of one man and one woman to the exclusion of all others'. In *Whiston v Whiston* [1995], the woman had committed bigamy, knowing that her first husband was still alive.

Maples v Maples [1987] illustrates that if a party has entered a valid marriage, then, in order to terminate that marriage and be able to enter another, the termination must also be valid.

Khan v UK [1986] 48 DR 253 – preventing multiple marriages in the UK is not a breach of Article 12.

Section 11(c)

The parties are not respectively male and female. The cases arising in this area normally concern a party who has undergone a sex change:

UK: *Corbett v Corbett* [1970], *Bellinger v Bellinger* [2001] (Declaration of Incompatibility of section 11 (c) MCA 1973 with the HRA 1998 Article 8 and 12 issued as a result of the facts in this case)

Europe: *Rees v UK* [1990], *Cossey v UK* [1991], *B v France* [1992], *Goodwin v UK* [2000]

As established in *Corbett*, the approach in England and Wales was to treat a transsexual as being of their original birth sex as recorded on the birth certificate, even if they had undergone full reassignment surgery, as the tests to be used related to chromosomal structures, etc. Following the European Court of Human Rights' decision in *Goodwin*, this will no longer be the case. Transsexuals who have completed reassignment surgery must be treated as their new sex for the purposes of marriage, if they have obtained a Gender Recognition Certificate under the Gender Recognition Act 2004 (GRA). To obtain such a certificate under section 9 GRA, the applicant must satisfy the following under section 2(1) GRA:

- they have or have had gender dysphoria;
- they have lived in their acquired gender for two years;
- they intend to live in their acquired gender until death;
- they produce the necessary proof required under the Act.

The evidence required is such to confirm the diagnosis of gender dysphoria, but reassignment surgery is not necessary.

In the event that the applicant is married when seeking a Gender Recognition Certificate, they can only be issued with an interim gender recognition certificate and must end their marriage to be able to obtain a full certificate.

A full gender recognition certificate enables a person to change the legal categorisation of their sex from male to female or female to male. As illustrated in *R (AB) v Secretary of State for Justice* [2009] where it was found to be unlawful to keep a woman with a full certificate in a man's prison.

Section 11(d)

In the case of a polygamous marriage entered into outside England and Wales, either party was, at the time of the marriage, domiciled in England or Wales.

Section 47 of the MCA 1973 allows matrimonial relief or a declaration concerning the validity of a marriage entered into under a law allowing polygamy (matrimonial relief includes nullity, divorce, judicial separation and matters relating to maintenance provisions). However, there have been cases where s 11(d) has not applied.

In *Radwan v Radwan (No 2)* [1973], the husband was domiciled in Egypt and married his first wife, an Egyptian domiciled woman, in Cairo. He later married his second wife, an English domiciled woman, in Paris, intending to enter into a polygamous marriage according to Egyptian law and to live in Egypt. They did live in Egypt, but later moved to, and became domiciled in, England. The second wife later petitioned for divorce.

The court held that, as the second marriage was valid in Egypt and they had intended to live there, it was valid in England. The court said that s 11(d) did not apply.

In *Hussain v Hussain* [1982], even though there was a potentially polygamous marriage, both parties had no capacity to marry again and s 11(d) did not apply; therefore, the marriage was valid.

VOIDABLE MARRIAGES

Voidable marriages exist in law but are defective, but it is for the parties involved to decide whether they will end the marriage. The marriage will continue until it is avoided by way of a decree.

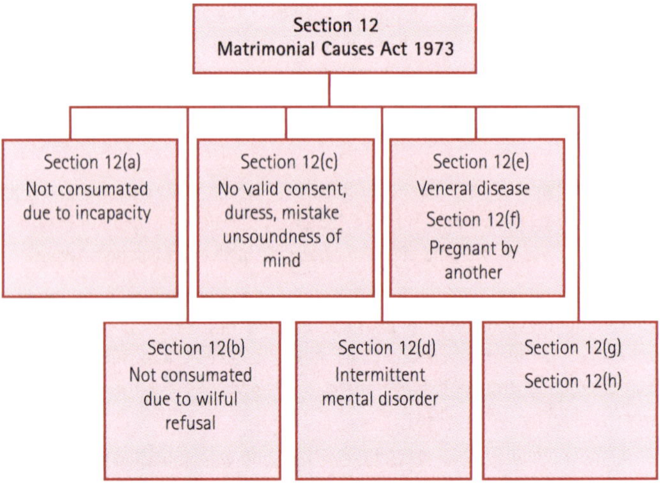

WHEN A VOIDABLE MARRIAGE ENDS

Section 16 of the MCA 1973 states that a decree of nullity granted after 31 July 1971 on the ground that a marriage is voidable will only annul the marriage with respect to any time after the decree has been made absolute. The marriage will be treated as if it had existed up to that time, notwithstanding the decree.

The grounds for voidability of marriages formed after 31 July 1971 are contained in s 12 of the MCA 1973.

Section 12(a)

The marriage has not been consummated owing to the incapacity of either party to consummate it.

SINGH v SINGH [1971] 2 WLR 963 S12(A)

A girl was persuaded by her parents to marry someone she did not choose to marry. After the marriage she failed to have anything to do with him and petitioned the courts for a decree of nullity under s 12(a) on the grounds that she could not consummate owning to her own incapacity.

The court held that to be successful under this section the inability to consummate must be more than a lack of attraction or dislike of the other person.

Section 12(b)

The marriage has not been consummated owing to the wilful refusal of the respondent to consummate it.

The difference in the wording of these grounds shows that, under s 12(a), a party can petition on his own incapacity but, under s 12(b), he cannot petition on his own wilful refusal.

Consummation occurs as soon as parties have sexual intercourse after the marriage. Sexual intercourse before marriage does not amount to consummation. The degree of sexual intercourse required was defined in *D v A* [1845] as being 'ordinary and complete and not partial and imperfect'. This was illustrated in *W v W* [1967], where it was stated that, as the husband was incapable of sustaining an erection, consummation did not occur.

Moreover, the inability must have a degree of permanence (*S v S* [1956]).

S v S [1956] P1

Both parties made genuine but unsuccessful attempts to consummate the marriage. The husband suggested that the wife should consult a doctor. Almost three years later the wife left the husband. The husband later sought a decree of nullity alleging that the wife was incapable of consummating the marriage or alternatively that she had wilfully refused to consummate the marriage. The wife consulted a doctor who diagnosed her with an abnormal hymen which could in his view be corrected by a minor surgical operation.

The court held that the true test of incapacity was the practical impossibility of consummation. A spouse must be regarded as incurable if the condition is only remedied by an operation involving an element of risk or danger. The court also ruled that in deciding whether a state of impotency was permanent the court must take into consideration future medical or surgical treatment which might remove the cause of the disability.

WILFUL REFUSAL

This is defined in *Horton v Horton* [1947] as 'a settled and definite decision come to without just excuse'.

This can arise in a number of ways, such as a psychological problem which does not amount to incapacity or the refusal to undergo an operation to remedy a physical defect preventing consummation. However, it must meet the definition, that is, it must be a settled and definite decision without just cause.

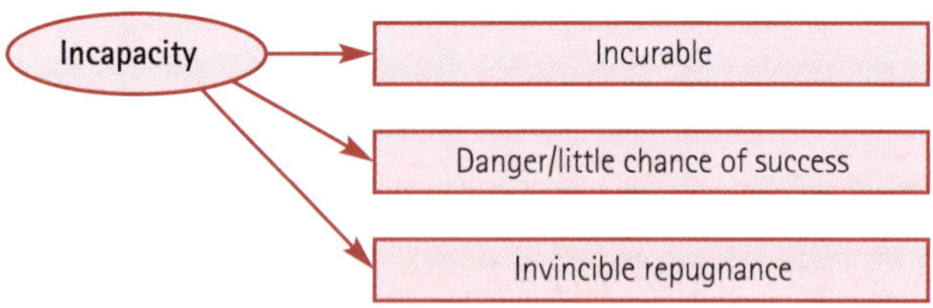

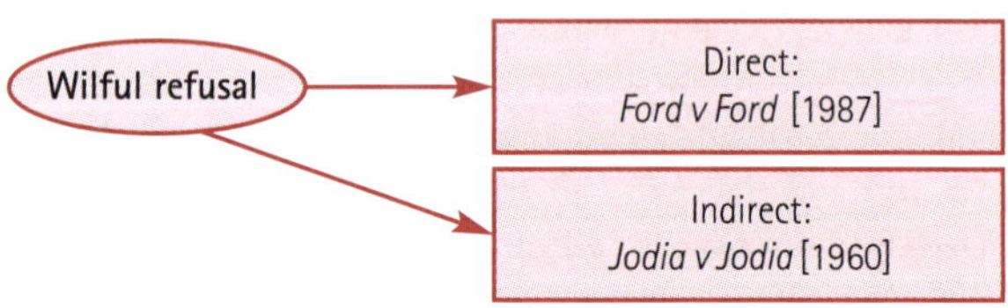

Section 12(c)

Lack of consent: either party did not validly consent, whether in consequence of duress, mistake, unsoundness of mind or otherwise.

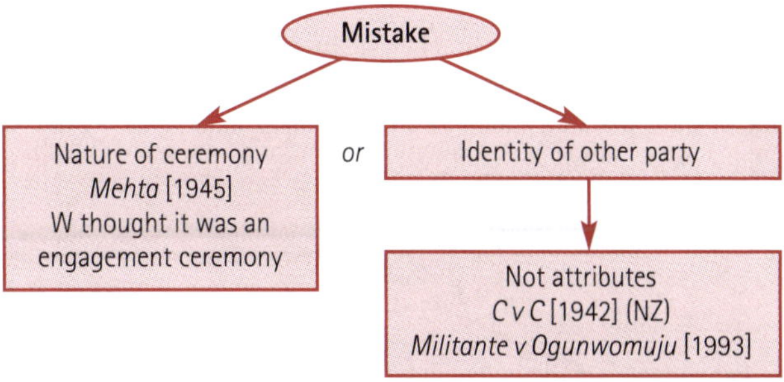

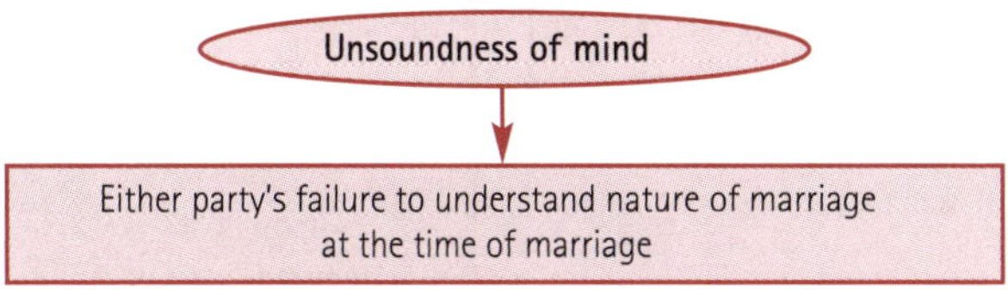

There is a presumption that, when a party enters into a marriage, he is capable of doing so and the burden of proof lies with the respondent.

Duress is said to be fear which is so overbearing that the element of free consent is absent.

In *Hirani v Hirani* [1982], the crucial question was 'Are the threats, pressure or whatever ... such as to destroy the reality of the consent and overbear the will of the individual.' It was held duress need not be fear of life or limb but the key to establishing duress was the effect of the actual threat rather than the nature of the threat. In this case the parents of their daughter threatened to completely disown her and remove her from her home if she failed to go through with the prearranged marriage. The fear of social ostracism was enough to find duress in this case.

SZECHTER v SZECHTER [1970] 3

It is generally accepted that a subjective test is to be applied in this situation, that is, 'has the petitioner been affected by the pressure?', not 'would an ordinary person of firm standing be affected?' (*Scott v Sebright* [1886]). In Scotland the courts have frequently applied this subjective test to arranged marriages where one of the parties has gone through the marriage ceremony due to family pressures and possible ostracism.

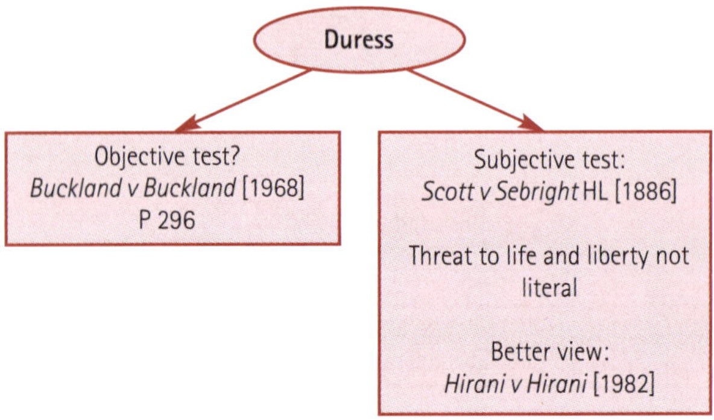

Section 12(c)

Consent obtained by duress – *P v R (Forced Marriage: Annulment: Procedure)* [2003]

The Forced Marriage (Civil Protection) Act 2007 is an important social reforming statute of power and humanity, protecting the basic right to marry by choice. This adds further support to Article 12 of the European Convention on Human Rights which protects the right to marry, which includes an individuals right not to be forced into a marriage.

This is a fundamental piece of legislation which recognises, for the first time, the difference between arranged marriages and forced ones. English courts can now provide injunctive relief to prevent such a marriage going ahead.

An early illustration of how the Act will work can be seen in the recent case involving an NHS doctor. The High Court in London issued an injunction under the Forced Marriage Act, demanding that Dr Abedin, an NHS doctor allegedly beaten, drugged and held captive by her family in Bangladesh, be returned to Britain. The court in Bangladesh was persuaded by the injunction and demanded her return to the UK.

Under section 63A(1) a forced marriage protection order (FMPO) made by a court may protect anyone:

- being forced into marriage;
- from any attempt to be forced into marriage; or
- already forced into marriage.

Further commentary on the impact of such orders is illustrated in *Re B (A Child) (Forced Marriage: Wardship: Jursdiction)* [2008]. *A Chief Constable v YK and Others* [2011] discusses the nature of a forced marriage and provides further guidance on the need for special advocates, the protection offered by court orders and whether knowledge held by police was sufficient to act in making an order.

Section 12(d)

This sub-section deals with a party suffering from a mental disorder. In this situation, a party can give valid consent and, because of this, the marriage cannot be voided by s 12(c). However, the party may not be fit for marriage because of the mental disorder.

The mental disorder, which can be continuous or intermittent, must be within the Mental Health Act 1983.

Section 12(e)

At the time of marriage, the respondent was suffering from VD in a communicable form.

Section 12(f)

At the time of the marriage, the respondent was pregnant by some person other than the petitioner.

Section 12(g)

This sub-section was added by virtue of the Gender Recognition Act 2004 and enables the marriage to be annulled on the basis that one of the parties to the marriage has obtained an interim gender recognition certificate. As highlighted earlier an interim certificate will be granted when there is a subsisting marriage, but all other requirements under the 2004 Act have been met. By commencing proceedings within a period of 6 months from the grant of the interim certificate, the party seeking to change gender can then apply for a full certificate.

Section 12(h)

This sub-section was also introduced by the Gender Recognition Act 2004 and enables a party to annul a marriage if they find out that the respondent is a person whose gender at the time of the marriage was an acquired gender under the 2004 Act. In other words if you discover after the marriage that your spouse has changed gender you can bring the marriage to an end using this provision.

BARS TO VOIDABLE

If the situation arises where the respondent wishes to prevent a decree of nullity being granted, the use of s 13 of the MCA 1973 must be considered.

Section 13(1)

This is considered to be a general bar to a voidable marriage. The court shall not grant a decree of nullity on the ground that a marriage is voidable if the respondent satisfies the court that:

(a) the petitioner, with knowledge that it was open to him to have the marriage voided, so conducted himself in relation to the respondent as to lead the respondent reasonably to believe that he would not seek to do so; and

(b) it would be unjust to the respondent to grant the decree.

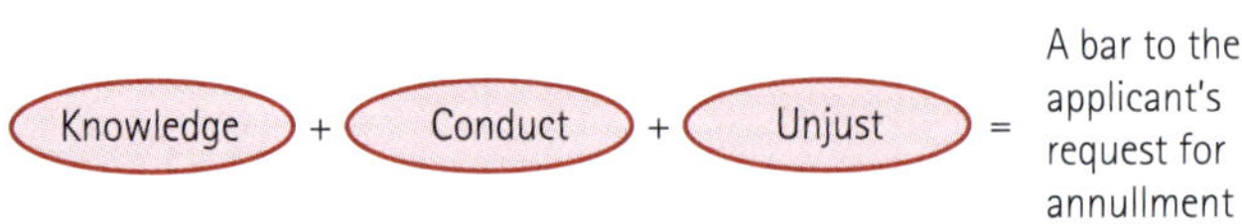

Section 13(2) MCA 1973

This is a more specific bar that links to the specific sub-sections detailed in section 12. Without prejudice to sub-s (1) above, the court shall not grant a decree of nullity by virtue of s 12 above on the grounds mentioned in paragraph (c), (d), (e), (f) or (h) of that section unless—

(a) it is satisfied that proceedings were instituted within the period of three years from the date of the marriage, or

(b) leave for the institution of proceedings after the expiration of that period has been granted under subsection (4) below.

(2A) Without prejudice to sub-s (1) above, the court shall not grant a decree of nullity by virtue of s 12 above on the ground mentioned in paragraph (g) of that section unless it is satisfied that proceedings were instituted within the period of six months from the date of issue of the interim gender recognition certificate.

Section 13(4) MCA 1973

In the case of proceedings for the grant of a decree of nullity by virtue of section 12 above on the grounds mentioned in paragraph (c), (d), (e), (f) or (h) of that section, a judge of the court may, on an application made to him, grant leave for the institution of proceedings after the expiration of the period of three years from the date of the marriage if:

(a) he is satisfied that the petitioner has at some time during that period suffered from mental disorder within the meaning of the Mental Health Act 1983, and

(b) he considers that in all the circumstances of the case it would be just to grant leave for the institution of proceedings.

(5) An application for leave under sub-s (4) above may be made after the expiration of the period of three years from the date of the marriage.

CHILDREN

Section 41 of the MCA 1973 applies to cases of nullity. This section requires the court to consider whether it should use its powers under the Children Act 1989 in relation to any children involved in the case.

FINANCIAL PROVISION

As a consequence of gaining a decree of nullity, whether due to the marriage being void or voidable, the parties are entitled to any of the financial and property orders available under the MCA 1973 (s 23 and s 24) that the court feels it appropriate to make. The orders will take effect on the granting of the decree.

The criteria that apply to the making of these orders are set out in s 25 of the MCA 1973 and are considered further in Chapter 3.

You should now be confident that you would be able to tick all of the boxes on the checklist at the beginning of this chapter. To check your knowledge of Nullity why not visit the companion website and take the Multiple Choice Question test. Check your understanding of the terms and vocabulary used in this chapter with the flashcard glossary.

2 Divorce

Ground for divorce

- Irretrievable breakdown s 1(1) MCA 1973
  - The five facts for Divorce s 1(2) MCA 1973
    - (1) Adultery s 1(2)(a) MCA 1973
    - (2) Behaviour s 1(2) (b) MCA 1973
    - (3) Desertion s 1(2) (c) MCA 1973
    - (4) Lived apart for a continuous period of at least two years s 1(2)(d) MCA 1973
    - (5) Lived apart for a continuous period of at least five years s 1(2)(e) MCA 1973

Defences to divorce

- living together for a period of 6 months after the event which forms the basis for the grounds of divorce
- s 5 grave financial hardship (only a defence to s 1(2)(e)) MCA 1973

Mediation

The Civil Partnership Act 2004

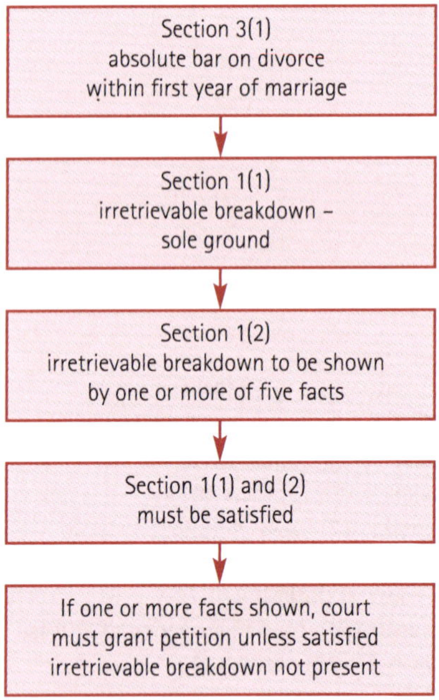

Under Part I Matrimonial Causes Act 1973 there is one sole ground on which a petition for divorce can be brought, that the marriage has irretrievably broken down (section 1(1) MCA 1973). In order to prove this, the petitioner must show the existence of one of five facts, which are under section 1(2) MCA 1973:

(a) the respondent has committed adultery and the petitioner finds it intolerable to live with the respondent;

(b) the respondent has behaved in such a way that the petitioner cannot reasonably be expected to live with the respondent;

(c) the respondent has deserted the petitioner for a continuous period of at least two years immediately preceding the presentation of the petition;

(d) the parties to the marriage have lived apart for a continuous period of at least two years immediately preceding the presentation of the petition … and the respondent consents to a decree being granted; or

(e) the parties to the marriage have lived apart for a continuous period of at least five years immediately preceding the presentation of the petition.

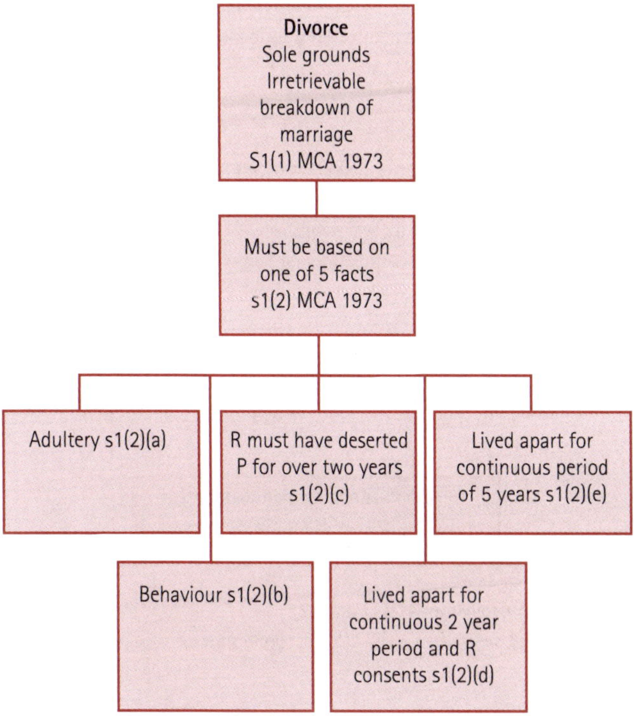

ADULTERY AND INTOLERABILITY

Section 1(2)(a)

The elements of the definition of adultery must be known. These must include that the respondent has committed adultery and that the petitioner finds it intolerable to live with the respondent.

ADULTERY

Voluntary sexual intercourse between a married person and a person of the opposite sex, who may or may not be married and who is not the other person's spouse.

The act must be voluntary (*Redpath v Redpath and Milligan* [1950]).

The degree of sexual intercourse required for adultery is that some degree of penetration is achieved (*Dennis v Dennis* [1955]). (This can be compared with the degree of sexual intercourse required for consummation, that is, 'ordinary and complete'.)

INTOLERABILITY

Adultery is considered to be a serious matrimonial offence and, as such, a standard of proof higher than the normal civil standard of proof is required (*Bastable v Bastable* [1968]). The subjective test can be satisfied by asking the petitioner do you find it intolerable to live with the respondent *Cleary v Cleary* [1974].

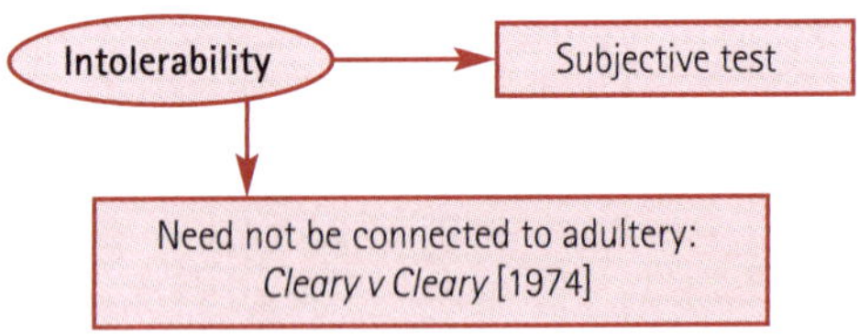

Reconciliation provision: s 2(1) and (2)

Cohabitation of over six months after becoming aware of adultery 'destroys' the fact.

BEHAVIOUR

Section 1(2)(b)

This fact is normally referred to as 'unreasonable behaviour'. However, the aspect of 'unreasonableness' must be considered in relation to whether or not the petitioner (P) is expected to live with the respondent (R), not to the standard of behaviour P must prove that R has behaved in such a way that P cannot reasonably be expected to live with R. The effect of R's behaviour is crucial *Ash v Ash* [1972].

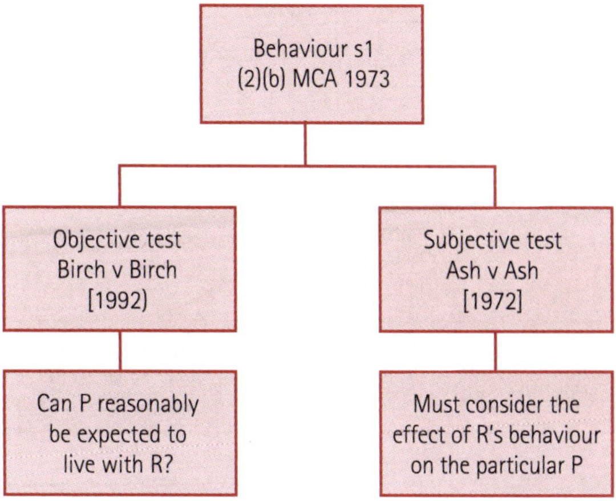

The test applied must have both elements. A subjective view should be taken of the petitioner's character and personality and an objective view of whether it is reasonable to expect her to live with the respondent: *Livingstone-Stallard v Livingstone-Stallard* [1974].

Case law demonstrates a wide range of grounds that constitute behaviour, even a series of minor incidents could be sufficient to justify this fact.

Lines v Lines (1963) unreasonable to expect a woman to tickle her husband's feet for hours each night.

O'Neill v O'Neill [1975] DIY enthusiast took eight months to replace toilet door.

Livingstone-Stallard v Livingstone-Stallard [1974] rudeness and constant criticisms.

Hadjimilitis (Tsavliris) v Tsavliris (Divorce: Irretrievable Breakdown) [2003] husband's constant criticisms, lack of warmth, controlling behaviour.

Reconciliation provisions

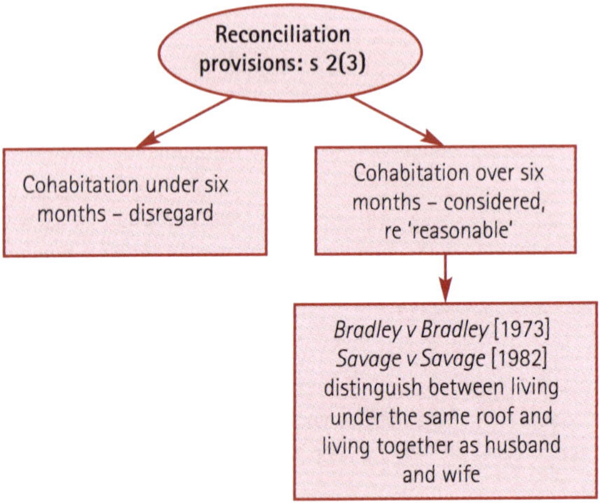

DESERTION

Section 1(2)(c)

There are said to be four requirements to prove the fact of desertion.

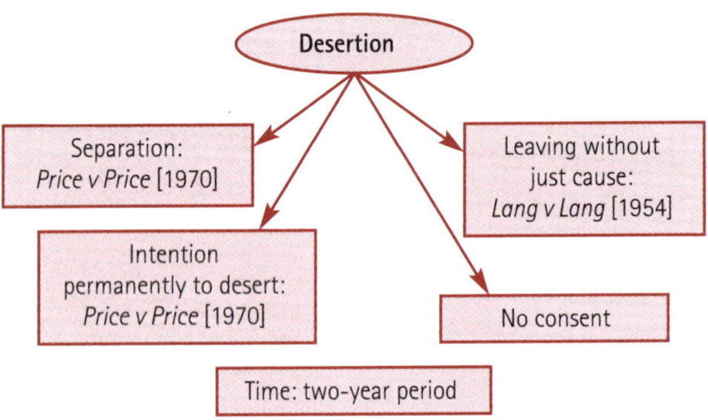

TERMINATION OF DESERTION

Absolute defences:

- the granting of a decree of judicial separation or a valid separation agreement. These are seen as supervening consent;
- the refusal of a reasonable offer of reconciliation without just cause, for example, a party offering reconciliation but attaching unreasonable conditions. In *Hutchinson v Hutchinson* [1963], there was to be no sexual intercourse: the husband was going to refuse sexual intercourse on the wife's return. This was held to be an unreasonable condition and the husband was held to be in constructive desertion;
- resumption of cohabitation which would amount to returning to a state of affairs where desertion would not have been found originally.

DISCRETIONARY DEFENCES

- Petitioner's implied consent to the separation by taking action to prevent the other spouse returning.
- Petitioner unsuccessfully petitioning for divorce or nullity on other grounds.

SEPARATION

Section 1(2)(d): two years' separation and respondent consents.

Section 1(2)(e): five years' separation.

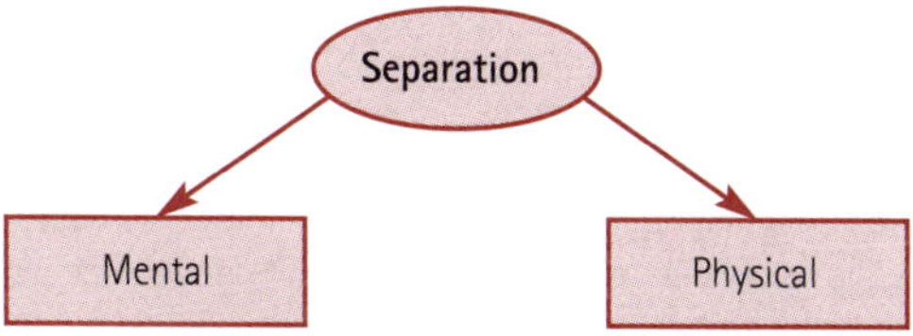

The recognition of the marriage being at an end can be made unilaterally and need not be communicated to the other spouse. It is clear that this could cause hardship, and the court will require evidence which shows when such a decision was reached. This could be by way of oral evidence, a letter or the ending of regular visits. However, if the court only has the oral evidence of the petitioner, it will treat such evidence with caution and look at the surrounding circumstances to see if there are any other indications as to when the period began.

SEPARATE HOUSEHOLDS

Section 2(6) states that a husband and wife shall be treated as living apart unless they are living with each other in the same household. This means that we have to consider the question of separate households under the same roof.

The essential element is that it can be shown that there has been a change in the nature of the relationship. This can best be illustrated by considering the cases of *Fuller v Fuller* [1973] and *Mouncer v Mouncer* [1972]. In *Fuller* the relationship changed to that of landlady and lodger, whereas in *Mouncer* the parties shared community of living (meals etc) and acted as a 'family'.

CONSENT

The essential difference in the facts of these cases concerns the requirement of consent by the respondent in s 1(2)(d) only.

The petitioner has the burden of showing that the respondent has consented in the proper manner. This consent must be expressed and is normally given via a signed statement. The respondent should be given sufficient information to enable him to give a proper consent to the decree.

The court will not imply any element of consent (*McGill v Robson* [1972]).

As with all matters of consent, there must be capacity (*Mason v Mason* [1972]). Again, it is for the petitioner to show that the respondent has this capacity if there is any doubt.

The respondent can withdraw his consent at any time prior to the decree nisi (r 7.31 (1)(a)) of the Family Proceedings Rules 2010. Also, under s 10(1) of the MCA 1973, the respondent may apply to the court at any time before decree absolute for the decree nisi to be rescinded if he can satisfy the court that he was misled by the petitioner, whether intentionally or not, on any matter which he took into consideration in giving his consent.

Once the five year separation under s 1(2)(e) has been proven to exist and has been acknowledged by the respondent, the respondent may not then attempt to petition or cross petition for divorce on any other fact (*Parsons v Parsons* [1975]).

TIME REQUIREMENTS

These are strictly applied, as shown by *Warr v Warr* [1975], and do not include the day of separation.

Reconciliation – under six months

↓

Time spent on reconciliation does not count towards the 2 or 5 year period and acts as an interruption to the time clock

Reconciliation – over 6 months

↓

Stops the time clock completely – any period of separation before the reconciliation cannot be counted. The parties must start the time clock again and separate for 2 or 5 years

PROVISIONS AFFECTING THE GRANTING OF DECREES

Section 5 MCA 1973

This defence is available only in cases based on the fact of five years' separation (s 1(2)(e)).

- Respondent could suffer grave financial *or* other hardship caused by the granting of the decree *and* it would in all the circumstances be wrong to dissolve the marriage.
- All elements need to be satisfied.

The application is made prior to the decree nisi and the court will consider all the circumstances of the case, including the conduct of the parties, their interests and the interests of any children or others.

GRAVE FINANCIAL HARDSHIP

Usually arises through loss of pensions for older wives, although note the extent of the court's powers to deal with the issue of pensions in Chapter 3.

- 'Grave' – ordinary meaning applied to all types of hardship – *Reiterbund v Reiterbund* [1974]; *Rukat v Rukat* [1975]
- Subjective view taken re particular marriage but objective view taken of 'grave' – *Rukat v Rukat* [1975]; *Mathias v Mathias* [1972]
- Hardship must be caused by the granting of the decree – *Talbot v Talbot* [1971]

Other payments may be made to compensate:

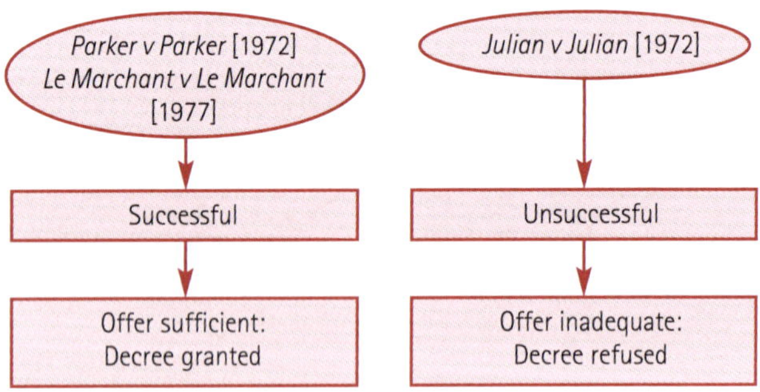

WRONG TO DISSOLVE THE MARRIAGE

Even if the respondent can show 'grave financial or other hardship', it is also necessary to show that it would be wrong to dissolve the marriage. In *Brickell v Brickell* [1973], the respondent's wife was able to show grave financial hardship but, because of her behaviour in spying on her husband and causing the failure of his business, it was held that it would not be wrong to dissolve the marriage. The decree was granted.

In light of the HRA 1998 (especially Articles 8 and 12) it is unlikely that a court would refuse to dissolve a marriage indefinitely.

Section 10 MCA 1973

In cases based on the facts in s 1(2)(d) and (e), the respondent can apply to the court for consideration of his financial provision on divorce. This provision is contained in s 10(2) of the MCA 1973. Section 10(3) empowers the court not to make the decree absolute unless it is satisfied that the respondent need not make any financial provision or that the provision made is reasonable and fair or the best that can be made in the circumstances.

In reaching its decision the court will have regard to the criteria set out in s 25 of the MCA 1973 and covered in Chapter 3.

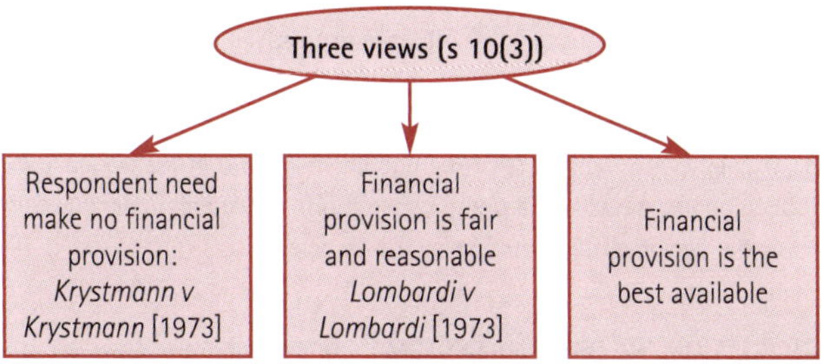

Garcia v Garcia [1992] covers past and future provisions.

The court can delay the granting of the decree absolute if it is not satisfied about financial arrangements.

Under s 10(4), the court can make the decree absolute, despite s 10(3), if the circumstances make it desirable to do so without delay or if it receives a satisfactory undertaking from the respondent that he will make financial provision for the petitioner that the court may approve.

The undertaking must not be vague, as the court must be able to enforce it. In the absence of specific proposals, the court will decide on an appropriate order.

Section 41 MCA 1973

This provision applies to all divorces where there are children involved. It does not depend on the application of the respondent. Under this provision, the court shall consider if there are any children of the family concerned and, where there are such children, whether, in the light of any proposed arrangements for the welfare of those children, it should exercise any of its powers under the Children Act 1989 in respect of any of them. However, the views of the children cannot prevent the marriage coming to an end.

DIVORCE PROCEDURE IN BRIEF

The manner in which a divorce is obtained has led to criticism of the law. The 'special procedure', which applies to all but defended divorces, enables the parties to obtain their decree without the need to attend court, and with the court's role limited to scrutiny of the divorce documentation. The petitioner will be required to file at court the divorce petition, to which the respondent files a response. If there is no question of a defence or cross petition, the petitioner also swears an affidavit as to the evidence relied on to prove the irretrievable breakdown of the marriage and the fact from s 1(2) of the MCA 1973. The district judge, if happy with the nature of the documents, and that the evidence in the petition supports the fact, will grant a decree nisi, and thereafter the petitioner can seek the decree absolute to finalise the divorce.

CRITICISMS OF THE PRESENT SYSTEM

Over recent years, there has been growing dissatisfaction with the law concerning divorce in this country and the seemingly ever increasing number of divorces, which now stands at approximately 153,000 per annum, according to the Judicial Statistics for 2004. The main criticisms of the present system are that it:

- allows marriages to be ended too quickly and easily without the parties having to have regard to the consequences and effects on others of their actions;
- does little to try and preserve marriages that are in difficulty;
- does little to try to diminish any adverse effects or trauma suffered by the children of the family;
- increases the bitterness and hostility between the parties;
- is misleading and confusing;
- is open to abuse. Adultery and behaviour are used in approximately 80 per cent of divorces, but often, false allegations are used to facilitate the granting of the divorce;

- can be used to distort the parties' bargaining positions, for example, where matters regarding children are being used as bargaining ploys.
  (*Family Law: The Ground for Divorce*, Law Com No 192, 1990)

The reforms suggested to overcome these difficulties were intended to:

- support and save marriages capable of being saved;
- enable those not 'saveable' to be dissolved with the minimum of distress, hostility and bitterness;
- encourage, as far as possible, the amicable resolution of matters concerning finance, housing, children and parties' responsibilities to each other;
- prevent or minimise the harm and distress to any children of the family during and after the divorce, and promote the continued sharing of parental responsibility and other responsibilities or duties towards the children.

The legislation that was brought forward by the government, the Family Law Act (FLA) 1996, while containing some of the Law Commission aims, placed emphasis on the methods to be used to reduce hostility and bitterness, to reduce the cost to the parties and the taxpayer, and to trying to reduce divorce by ensuring that the parties were fully informed as to the nature of the process.

Part II of the FLA 1996, which was intended to replace the MCA 1973 with regards to divorce and the procedure for divorcing has not been brought in to force and it is clear that the government's intention is not to implement it. What has remained of the reforms is the process of mediation.

MEDIATION

Mediation was seen as integral to the new divorce process under the FLA 1996 and the intention to reduce the harmful and distressing effects of divorce. By enabling couples to reach their own arrangements as to the future, improve communications between them and increase the chances for co-operation in relation to children, the aim was to remove the adversarial nature of the MCA system. In addition, given that the resolution of disputes would be 'party led', this would also lead to a reduction in the amount of state funding used in paying lawyers. Mediation was seen as being a method of reducing the number of divorces, since it would leave the door open to reconciliation. This confusion between the concepts of mediation and reconciliation was unfortunate, since mediation is not primarily focused on saving the marriage, but on helping move the parties forward into life as a divorced individual, and perhaps may explain the lack of take-up of mediation services. Additionally, the fact that legal advice would still be needed, if only to draw up the resulting agreement for ratification by the court, may have hindered the scale of mediation take-up since the parties may have preferred to stay with their lawyer, rather than deal with two different services.

Part III of the FLA 1996 operated to introduce mediation to the process of divorce by way of amendments to the Legal Aid Act 1988. This Act has since been repealed by the Access to Justice Act 1990, and the mediation requirements for family disputes are now found in the Funding Code, published by the Legal Services Commission, which sets out the detailed criteria for the granting of state funding under this latter Act. The Code sets out the nature of proceedings which will be subject to mediation in para 2.2, and this includes (*inter alia*) matters under:

- the MCA 1973;
- the Adoption Act 1976;
- the Children Act 1989 (Parts I, II and III); and
- the FLA 1996 (Part IV).

Hence, if a party to any of the specified 'family matters' requires state funding, they will have to be assessed for suitability for mediation as a means to resolve the dispute, rather than being granted state funding for purely legal representation. The Funding Code sets out the procedure to be applied, and also establishes the situations where an assessment for mediation suitability is not appropriate. An applicant for state funding will not be required to undergo a mediation assessment:

- if the proceedings are under s 37 MCA 1973;
- if the proceedings are under the Inheritance (Provision for Family and Dependants) Act 1975;
- where it is in the interests of justice that legal representation be granted as a matter of urgency and the criteria for emergency representation are satisfied;

- where there is no mediator available to the applicant or any party to the proceedings to hold the assessment meeting;
- where the mediator is satisfied that mediation is not suitable to the dispute because another party to the dispute is unwilling to attend an assessment meeting with a mediator to consider mediation;
- where family proceedings are already in existence and the client is a respondent to the proceedings and there are less than eight weeks to the court hearing date; and
- where the applicant has a reasonable fear of domestic abuse from a potential party to the mediation and is therefore unwilling and fearful of mediating with them. (Funding Code Procedure paras C28 and C29.)

If the applicant does not fall within one of the above categories, they will have to attend a meeting with the mediator to see if the dispute is capable of mediation. In the event that the matter is suitable, the applicant will be granted state funding for the purposes of mediation, to include legal representation in the drawing up of any agreement following mediation. Should mediation be deemed unsuitable, the applicant will be considered for state funding for legal representation. Suitability will require consideration by the mediator carrying out the assessment of factors such as the nature of the dispute, the parties' attitudes and all the circumstances of the case.

As with the previous legal aid scheme, applicants will also be considered on their financial eligibility. If the applicant is required to contribute to their funding, this contribution will apply regardless of whether they are undergoing mediation, or are receiving legal advice. There also exists the statutory charge in relation to mediation. Hence where property is recovered or preserved for the state funded party as a result of mediation, a sum equal to the fees incurred will be a first charge on that property in favour of the Legal Services Commission (the body that now administers state funding).

Should mediation be deemed appropriate following the assessment meeting and then fail to resolve the issue, the applicant may request state funding for legal assistance. This request will require additional consideration of the reasons for the failure of mediation and whether the applicant behaved reasonably throughout the mediation. If mediation fails, it cannot be assumed that funding for legal advice will then be granted.

The efficacy of mediation compared to legal advice and representation has been considered by Gwynn Davis *et al.*, *Monitoring Publicly Funded Family Mediation* (2000). While it was concluded that mediation does have a value, it is not always as cost effective as legal advice alone, nor does it achieve resolution of the dispute. Hence it may be questioned why all applicants for state funding should be pushed in the direction of mediation. It is also worth noting that many mediators expect the client to have access to legal advice during mediation since a mediator cannot advise or suggest outcomes. If a client requires state funding for mediation, how will they then be able to afford a lawyer as well? See 'Collaborative Law' below for an additional option.

In April 2010 the new Family Procedure Rules (FPR) 2010 came into force. The FPR introduce a new set of rules and procedures for dealing with all family law cases. The rules have an overriding objective similar to that used in civil cases with the exception of the provision in respect of welfare issues. The overriding objective at Rule 1.1 states 'these rules are a new procedural code with the overriding objective of enabling the court to deal with cases justly, having regard to any welfare issues involved.' The aim is for cases to be dealt with as expeditiously, fairly and as proportionately as possible, ensuring all parties are on an equal footing and that costs are minimised where possible. To this end Practice Direction 3A has been introduced to ensure all applicants have considered alternative dispute resolution prior to making an application for a court order. All separating couples will be expected to attend a Mediation Information Assessment Meeting. It is hoped this practice direction will encourage all parties to have considered the use of mediation as an alternative means of resolving their dispute and so avoid court-litigated settlement.

COLLABORATIVE LAW

A new process introduced by groups of solicitors specifically trained in collaborative law processes to assist parties in reaching agreement on separation without the need to go to court. This scheme provides what mediation could not, legal advice. The process works by each party meeting with their own solicitor to explain what they are seeking from the settlement process. The solicitors then meet or discuss by phone the best way to approach the first meeting. A four-way face-to-face meeting with both sides and their lawyers present then takes place. Each party to the process signs an agreement agreeing to negotiate a settlement via the collaborative process and without the need to go to court.

The process aims to include discussions about children as well as resolving financial settlements. Negotiations are conducted face to face to resolve each side's issues and this helps to avoid lengthy litigation processes conducted by letter. At the final meeting an agreement detailing settlement for both sides is drawn up and signed by the parties. The aim of the process is to avoid the adversarial approach, keep costs down and resolve issues according to how quickly the parties wish to progress (Resolution). This process is very distinct and separate from mediation. The process is also supported by the judiciary *S v P (Settlement by Collaborative Law Process)* [2008].

THE CIVIL PARTNERSHIP ACT 2004

This Act, which came into force in 2005, is designed to enable same sex couples to register their partnership and, as a result, benefit from similar rights afforded to married couples. The Act operates therefore in a similar way to the laws of marriage and divorce, although the law is very clear same sex couples cannot enter into a marriage. This was discussed at length in *Wilkinson v Kitzinger* [2006].

WHO CAN REGISTER THE PARTNERSHIP?

To register a partnership the following must be satisfied:

- the couple must be same sex;
- they cannot be married or in an existing registered partnership;
- they must be over 16 years old (if under 18 parental consent must be given);
- they must not be in the prohibited degrees of relationship (s 3);
- they must give the prescribed notice to the Superintendent Registrar (s 8);
- they must sign the register in the presence of a registered person and before two witnesses (s 2).

Note: there is no requirement under the Act that the couple live together before or after registration, although it is assumed that this will be the case. The Equality Act 2010, section 202 proposes changes to the Civil Partnership Act 2004 that will allow civil partnership ceremonies to be held in religious buildings or as part of a religious ceremony, although this provision is not yet in force.

The partnership may be held to be void or voidable on the basis of criteria that reflect the same provisions in the Matrimonial Causes Act 1973 with the exception of consummation. The grounds for a partnership to be declared void can be found under section 49 CPA 2004 and under section 50 CPA 2004 if the partnership is voidable.

CONSEQUENCES OF REGISTRATION

The main consequences mirror those of marriage – hence once a partnership has been registered, it can only be ended by order of the court (s 44 CPA 2004). To dissolve the partnership the court must be satisfied that:

- The partnership has broken down irretrievably and that one of the specified facts is proven. The facts to be proven are as follows. However note adultery is not available as a fact on which to prove irretrievable breakdown, although a petitioner would use behaviour in this instance.

  The facts are:

  - The respondent has behaved in such a way that the applicant cannot reasonably be expected to live with the respondent.
  - The couple have lived apart for a period of 2 years and the respondent consents to the order.
  - The couple have lived apart for a period of 5 years.

It is assumed that the courts will interpret separation in the same way as for divorce.

FINANCIAL CONSEQUENCES

If the partnership is avoided or dissolved under s 44 each party has a right to claim maintenance as if a spouse (s 72 and Sched 5). In addition, s 65 provides that where one of the partners has made significant contribution towards the improvement of property, where both or only one of the partners have a beneficial interest, the court can grant an interest or a larger share, to the contributing partner, hence avoiding the need to take proceedings via land law and the concept of resulting or constructive trust.

You should now be confident that you would be able to tick all of the boxes on the checklist at the beginning of this chapter. To check your knowledge of Divorce why not visit the companion website and take the Multiple Choice Question test. Check your understanding of the terms and vocabulary used in this chapter with the flashcard glossary.

3

Financial remedies and orders on divorce

Financial provision during marriage may be necessary where the parties are separated but not yet divorced.

Under s 2 Domestic Proceedings and Magistrates' Courts Act 1978, the Family Proceedings Court in the Magistrates' Court may make any one or more of the following orders:

1 An order requiring the respondent's periodical payments

2 Lump sum

3 Periodical payments to a child of the family or for the benefit of a child of the family

4 Lump sum to a child of the family or for the benefit of a child of the family

Section 3 DPMCA lists factors the court should take into account and these are similar to the s 25 MCA 1973 factors.

These cases were previously referred to as claims for ancillary; however, the introduction of the new Family Proceedings Rules 2010 in April 2011 has changed the terms used. Part 9 Applications for Financial Remedy of the FPR, Rule 2.30 refers to the generic term of financial remedies or more specifically financial orders. These orders relate to the distribution of financial and property assets between the parties after divorce, nullity (where a decree has been sought) or judicial separation, and include claims for children. The statutory provisions are the same, regardless of the extent of those assets, but in many so called 'big money cases' the court's discretion is much wider.

MCA 1973: TYPES OF FINANCIAL ORDERS

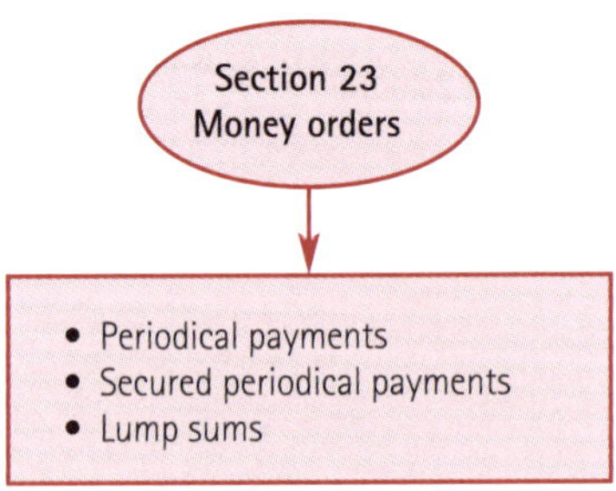

1 Maintenance pending suit

2 Periodical payments

3 Lump sum orders

4 Transfer of property orders

5 Settlement of property

6 Sale of property

7 Child orders

8 Pension sharing

ISSUES IN RELATION TO THESE ORDERS

- Secured orders will survive the death of the payer.
- Both secured and unsecured periodical payments orders cease on the remarriage of the payee.
- Periodical payments may be varied, up or down.
- Periodical payments may be ordered to cease in the event of cohabitation for a defined period.
- Lump sum orders provide money up front, therefore later remarriage is irrelevant.
- A lump sum can be ordered to be paid in instalments.
- A lump sum can be invested to provide income.

In *McFarlane v McFarlane* [2006]; *Parlour v Parlour* [2004] the Court of Appeal ruled that periodical payments of a short duration can be used to create a capital fund and lead to a clean break. However, the House of Lords said that this was the wrong approach and would be unfair to the wife. Periodical payments of unlimited duration were ordered with the onus on the husband to apply for variation in the future if the circumstances changed.

MILLER v MILLER; MCFARLANE v MCFARLANE [2006] 1 FLR 1186

In *McFarlane* the wife had given up her highly paid and successful career as a solicitor to look after the children. Unusually in this case there was far more income available than there was capital. The Court of Appeal had replaced the trial Judge's joint lives order for income, with a 5 year order. The Court of Appeal had treated the surplus of income over expenditure as giving the wife simply a means by which the wife could build up capital reserves. But the House of Lords said that this was a wrong approach: 'in the present case a 5 year order is most unlikely to be sufficient to achieve a fair outcome', and moreover, putting the onus on the wife to come back to court for variation before the 5 years had elapsed was not fair. It should be the husband who should have to come back to apply for a variation. Therefore they overturned the 5 year limit and once again made a joint lives order.

In *Miller* the wife received a lump sum of £5m. The marriage had only lasted approximately three years, so there was no reason for equality of division. However, the husband had gained hugely in wealth during the marriage and the wife had given up a good job, so she got 1/6th of his total assets capitalised as a lump sum.

Subsequently, Mrs M appealed successfully. Her application to extend and/or capitalise periodical payments was successful. The court ordered periodical payments payable to the wife until 2015 based on percentages of his income rising if he earns more.

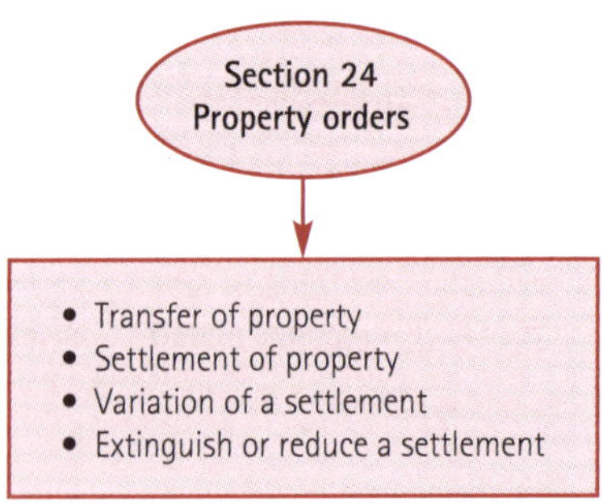

ISSUES IN RELATION TO THESE ORDERS

- Transfers of property interest may be coupled with a lump sum payment to compensate for the loss of a capital asset.
- The compensation may take the form of a charge over the property removing access to capital for one party.
- Maintenance for children may not be offset against a capital transfer.
- Settling property until a specified event (eg the children reaching 18) may delay the sale and division of equity too much, resulting in one or both of the parties being unable to rehome.
- A settlement linked to remarriage or cohabitation may impact negatively on any children.
- None of these orders is consistent with a clean break. See *Lauder v Lauder* [2007] 2 FLR 802 where the wife obtained an upward variation of her periodical payments 19 years after the divorce!

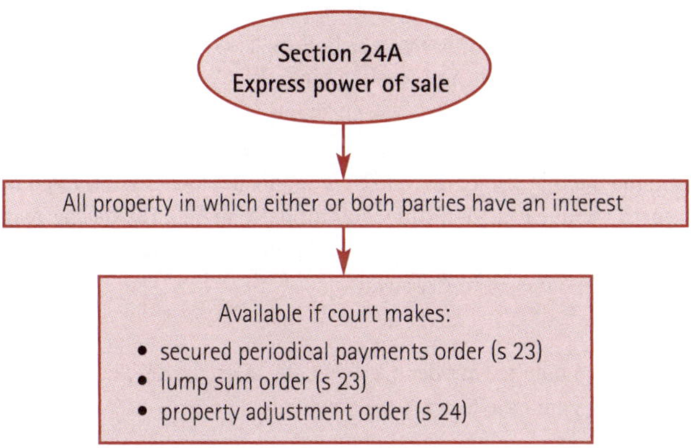

ISSUES IN RELATION TO THESE ORDERS

- promotes the clean break;
- final order therefore certain;

- normally suitable in big money cases or where couples do not have dependent children.

CONSIDERATIONS FOR THE COURT

When dealing with ancillary relief claims, the court is required to look at a range of factors as set out in s 25 MCA 1973. The court does, however, have a wide discretion in dealing with the matrimonial assets.

GENERAL CONSIDERATIONS

The clean break (s 25A)

The idea behind these provisions is to bring to an end any dependence or obligation between the parties as soon as is practicable, depending on the circumstances of the case (*Suter v Suter and Jones* [1987] 2 All ER 336).

SUTER v SUTER AND JONES [1987] 2 ALL ER 336

The Court of Appeal considered the s 25A clean break principle in this case. The court took the view that in cases where there are very young children, as in this case, a clean break order is not appropriate despite the fact that the husband was of very little means. Instead the Court of Appeal made only a nominal order so as not to end the possibility of increased periodical payments if circumstances changed in the future. Additionally the court said the man with whom the wife was cohabiting could be expected to contribute towards the household expenses.

The court has a duty to consider a 'clean break' in each case (*Barrett v Barrett* [1988]). It does not have to apply the provisions.

THE STARTING POINT

In exercising its discretion, the court should use a 'starting point' to assist in establishing what would be the appropriate distribution. A variety of approaches have been favoured in the past by the courts, however, the leading case of *White v White* [2000] states that the starting point is to focus on the needs of the parties as measured against the yardstick of equality. However, this must now be looked at in light of *Miller; McFarlane* [2006].

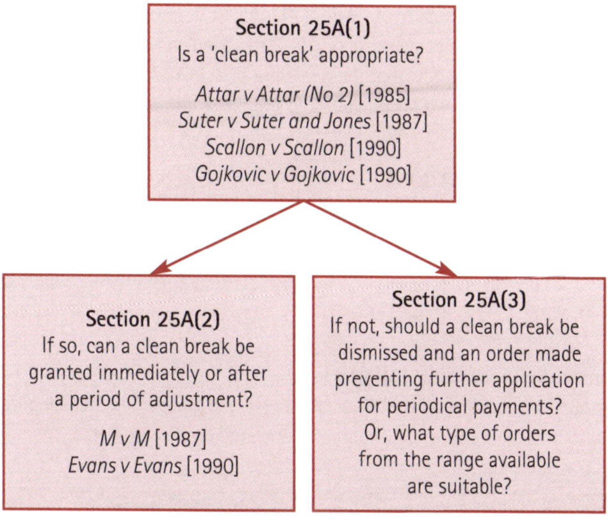

WHITE v WHITE [2000] 2 FLR 981

The parties were very wealthy people and had been married for over 20 years. The case concerned division of property rather than periodical payments, but it made an important universal statement of principle, namely that parties to a marriage should be treated with fairness and there should be a starting point of equality of treatment:

> . . . In seeking to achieve a fair outcome, there is no place for discrimination between husband and wife and their respective roles . . . whatever the division of labour chosen by the husband and wife, or forced upon them by circumstances, fairness requires that this should not prejudice or advantage either party.
>
> Lord Nicholls

The approach of the court will differ if it is a big money case – where there are sufficient assets to go round. The courts must test the proposed division of assets with the yardstick of equality to ensure that the parties are not being discriminated against, with the wife suffering as a result of being a home-maker rather than a business person as approved in *Charman v Charman* [2007]. This would suggest that the one-third principle as applied in *Duxbury v Duxbury* [1990] is now out of favour and should be discounted.

SPECIFIC CONSIDERATIONS

The welfare of minor children of the family (s 25(1) of the MCA 1973)

The welfare of the children *is not paramount* under the MCA and will not override other considerations. However, it is the first and most important consideration (*Suter v Suter and Jones* [1987]; *C v C (Financial Provision: Short Marriage)* [1997]).

Financial resources (s 25(2)(a))

The court will consider all the financial resources of the parties, including those likely to arise in the future. All sources of income will be considered.

Court looks at the reality of the situation: *Hardy v Hardy* [1981]; *Newton v Newton* [1990]

↓

The future must be considered – increase or decrease in earning capacity: *Mitchell v Mitchell* [1984]; *Parlow v Parlow* [2004]

↓

Potential payer must have means to pay: *Brown v Brown* [1981]

↓

New partner's income will only be considered as the effect of releasing more of the payer's resources for any orders to be made: *Martin v Martin* [1977]; *Frary v Frary* [1993]

↓

The source of the resource: *White v White* [2000]

Financial needs, obligations and responsibilities (s 25(2)(b))

As a direct corollary of income and resources, the court will consider what needs, obligations and responsibilities the parties will have now and in the future.

Needs are assessed on a subjective basis: *Leadbeater v Leadbeater* [1985]; *Dart v Dart* [1996]

↓

The party keeping the children will have future obligations until they become independent: *Mesher v Mesher* [1980]

↓

New families may need to be maintained as well as the former families. The court will attempt to balance the demands of both: *Stockford v Stockford* [1982]

↓

The resources of the new partner may be taken into account: *K v K* (Periodical Payment: Cohabitation) [2006] 2 FLR 468

K v K (Periodical Payment: Cohabitation) [2006] 2 FLR 468

The wife had deliberately not married her new partner so that she would continue to receive her periodical payments, but clearly intended remaining with him and had her finances entangled with his. The Court of Appeal held that cohabitation cannot be ignored and the wife should strive for financial independence from her husband. Financial commitment is an illustration of overall, including emotional, commitment, whether a couple are married or cohabiting. On the facts payments should not terminate altogether, but the judge could see no reason why a court order should not terminate on cohabitation after a certain period, as it would better reflect modern society.

MESHER v MESHER [1980] 1 ALL ER 126

An order for sale of the property should take effect from when the youngest child reached 17. This case introduced what is commonly known as a Mesher order. However, a Mesher order has now developed so as to include other triggers for orders for sale. For example, specific events regarding children, e.g. be 18 as the age of majority, or finishing full-time education including university, or when the youngest leaves school or where the wife dies or remarries. More recently these types of orders have been used to include clauses regarding fact specific clauses such as cohabitation. When the trigger event happens the property is sold and both spouses receive their share of the proceeeds.

Martin Orders

This is an order named after the decision in *Martin v Martin* [1977] and is similar to a Mesher order. A Martin order allows a spouse to remain in the family home until a trigger event occurs that relates to the occupying spouse. This type of event may include remarriage, death or cohabitation. When the court orders a Mesher or Martin order it can often prevent the parties from achieving the much sought after clean break.

Standard of living (s 25(2)(c))

When dealing with wealthy families, it is often possible for the court to settle matters without any significant drop in living standards. The court will consider the standard of living to which the parties have become accustomed and will seek to maintain that standard.

However, for the majority of couples, it is not possible for one household to become two without some drop in the standard of living. While the courts can try to apportion this reduction evenly, if there are dependent children this is not always feasible.

Ages of the parties and duration of marriage (s 25(2)(d))

The ages of the parties can have an effect on the orders made – it is much more common for young couples without children to be able to make a clean break from each other. If both are employed, the court may not need to make an order for maintenance/property adjustment at all.

However, in *C v C (Financial Provision: Short Marriage)* [1997], even though the marriage only lasted for nine months, the wife was given a large award because of the presence of a young child and her fragile state of health.

An older couple, especially with a long marriage, are likely to need more far reaching orders, particularly if the wife has given up a career to raise children and be a home-maker. She will be at an age where a career is unobtainable, and her devotion to the family needs compensating (*L v L* [2002]; *Charman v Charman* [2007] 1 FLR 1246).

The courts will not normally equate marriage and cohabitation unless there is a significant degree of commitment: *Kokosinski v Kokosinski* [1980]. However, where pre-marital cohabitation runs seamlessly into marriage then that cohabitation must be taken into account: *CO v CO* [2004] 1 FLR 1095 – 8 years cohabitation and 4 years marriage equated to 12 years duration.

Heather Mills v Sir Paul McCartney [2008] EWHC (Fam)
Despite Heather Mills' attempts to argue the marriage was over 6 years in age, the judge found that although the parties met in 1999 and formed a relationship, the parties did not cohabit from March 2000 but did so from the date of the marriage (11 June 2002). The parties separated in April 2006. The length of the marriage was just under 4 years.

Physical or mental disability (s 25(2)(e))
Allowances will be made for disability if it is possible to compensate by monetary means. If the disability worsens, then allowances will be made: *Sakkas v Sakkas* [1987].

Contributions to the family welfare (s 25(2)(f))
Contributions to the welfare of the family traditionally concentrate on the role played by the wife in raising the children. However, other types of contribution are just as relevant, and in particular, the contribution of building the family business and being an excellent money-maker are frequently cited. In *White v White* [2000] and *L v L* [2002] the courts have made clear that 'domestic contributions' should not be undervalued simply because they cannot be assessed/costed in the same way as economic activity.

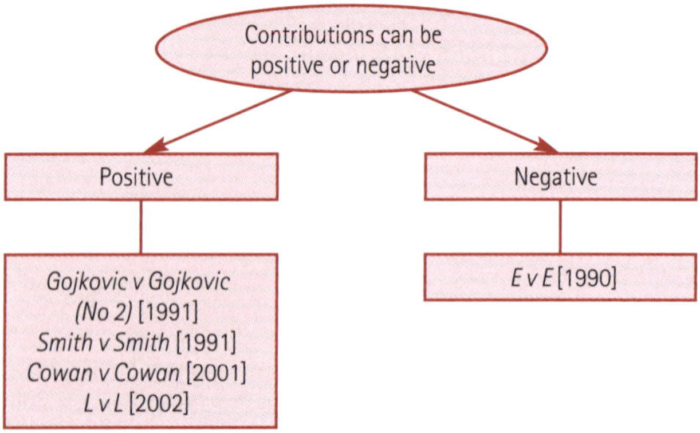

Conduct that would be inequitable to disregard (s 25(2)(g))

The courts are reluctant to examine the parties' conduct: *E v E* [1990].

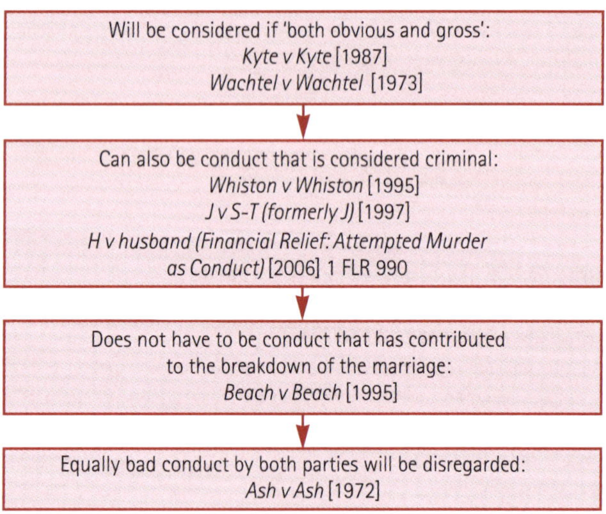

H v HUSBAND (FINANCIAL RELIEF: ATTEMPTED MURDER AS CONDUCT) [2006] 1 FLR 990

The husband had attacked the wife, who was a police officer, in the home, and was sentenced to 12 years for her attempted murder. She was unable to work after the incident, which was witnessed by their then 5 year old twins. The wife left the home as she could not cope with the memories. The Court held that the wife should get the matrimonial home and the bulk of the assets. The reason being that it was because of the husband's criminal conduct that the parties found themselves in the position they were in.

Loss of future benefit (s 25(2)(h))

The main benefit to be considered under this provision is the loss of pension entitlement as a spouse of the pension holder (*Parker v Parker* [1972]; *Brooks v Brooks* [1995]). Following various amendments to the MCA 1973 the court has a range of options available to it:

- **Set-off**: the court can make an increased lump sum order or deal with the matrimonial property so as to give the non-pension holder a greater share, thus compensating for the loss of pension benefits.
- **Pension attachment orders**: the court, under s 25B, C and D, can direct that a specified portion of the pension shall be paid to the spouse on the retirement of the pension holding spouse. No funds will be transferred prior to retirement. Assumes that the pension holding spouse will reach retirement age.
- **Pension sharing orders**: the court, under s 21A and s 24B, C and D, can direct that a specified portion of the pension shall be transferred immediately to the non-pension holding spouse, to hold in their own pension fund. The fund may then be transferred to other pension providers, additional contributions added and payments will commence on the retirement of the recipient spouse.

However, even though these orders are available, any order will be at the court's discretion and will only be made after consideration of the factors in s 25: *T v T (Financial Relief: Pensions)* [1998].

- **Pre-nuptial contracts**: *Crossley v Crossley* [2008] *The Times*, January 3. The Court of Appeal has now left the door open for the consideration of pre-nuptial contracts in ancillary relief. The case was one of a short marriage (3 years) and no children. Both parties were wealthy. Thorpe LJ: 'if ever there is to be a paradigm case in which the courts will look to the prenuptial agreement as not simply one of the peripheral factors but a factor of magnetic importance, then this is such a case'.

English law has been very resistant in recognising pre-nuptial agreements. The case of *Crossley* has, for the first time, taken a step towards doing so in certain cases. These possible circumstances are where both parties took legal advice before entering the agreement and circumstances have not changed since the agreement was signed or any changes that have arisen were foreseen and allowed for by the agreement. However since *Crossley* was decided the law has progressed further still and this is evidenced by the decision in *Radmacher v Grantino* [2010].

RADMACHER V GRANTINO [2010] UKSC 42

Katrina Radmacher and Nicolas Grantino both signed a pre-nuptial agreement prior to their marriage with the wife being the wealthier party. The agreement stated N would not benefit either directly or indirectly through any future children from K's wealth and similar provisions were added in respect any wealth N should acquire. Upon divorce K sought to reply on the agreement.

In a majority ruling with only Baroness Hale dissenting, the Supreme Court ruled at para 75 'The court should give effect to a nuptial agreement that is freely entered into by each party with a full appreciation of it's implications unless in the circumstances prevailing it would not be fair to hold the parties to their agreement.' The court further added 'the agreement would only carry weight if the parties enter into it of their own free will, without undue influence or pressure' at para 68 and the agreement was fair. Considerations of fairness will take account of the provision made for children. Each of these principles is fact dependent and was determined on the particular facts of this case. It was agreed a prenuptial agreement could be accorded weight in certain circumstances and as part of the discretionary process adopted by section 25 MCA 1973. N's appeal was therefore unsuccessful.

Despite the fact this type of situation applies to a minority, the Law Commission issued a consultation paper Marital Property Agreements in January 2011. This paper outlines the current legal position following the decision in *Radmacher*, proposals for reform of the law including the formalities required for effect to be given to such agreements and the advantages and disadvantages of reforming the law.

Section 31 of the MCA 1973: variation of orders

The court's powers are very wide in this area, but there are certain orders that cannot be varied. These are seen to be made in full and final settlement. They are:

- property adjustment orders;
- lump sum orders (unless ordered to be paid in instalments).

Usually, the need for a variation arises because of a change in circumstances of either the paying or receiving spouse. Examples are where the paying spouse has taken on the responsibilities of a second family; the receiving spouse has increased needs; or there has been an increase or decrease in the paying spouse's income. When considering applications for variation, the court shall have regard to all the circumstances of the case, including any changes in those circumstances, the first consideration being the welfare of a minor child of the family.

The court has to decide whether to vary the order for a limited period under s 31(7). The court's attitude is similar to that of a clean break, that is, it is often reluctant to terminate an order altogether. The court has to consider whether or not the payee would be able to adjust to the new circumstances without undue hardship, and a major factor in its judgment would be any future uncertainty.

The approach of the courts is often to refuse to terminate the order, instead reducing it to a nominal order so that, if the payee's circumstances were to deteriorate, he could apply for a further variation and the existence of the nominal order could be seen as a safeguard. It is also of note that the court can, on an application for variation, make a lump sum order or a property adjustment order, if they feel that this is the most appropriate way of dealing with the case, even though the variation request is in relation to a periodical payment order.

It should be remembered that, where the parties have agreed on the financial matters and consent orders have been made, the limitations regarding lump sums and property adjustment orders still apply; also, if a variation of a consent order is sought, then it will be necessary to show at least some of the following factors:

- fresh evidence coming to light which was not known at the time the order was made;
- the parties, including the court, relied on erroneous information;
- fraud or non-disclosure, the absence of which would have led to a substantially different order;
- exceptionally, the basis for the original order has been destroyed.

In order to avoid these hurdles, parties may appeal against an order out of time. However, there are strict limitations on this course of action and leave will only be granted if the applicant can meet the requirements laid down in *Barder v Barder* [1987].

Following a clean break order the wife retained the home to occupy with the couple's children. Shortly after settlement the wife killed the children and then committed suicide. The issue for consideration was that the wife's will left the property to her mother. The House of Lords then laid down the principles under which the husband would be allowed to appeal out of time. These requirements are that:

- new events invalidate the basis of the order and an appeal would be likely to succeed;
- the new event occurred within a few months of the order;
- the application is made reasonably promptly; and
- the appeal, if granted, would not prejudice third parties who had acted in good faith and for valuable consideration on the basis of the order.

The main reason for such a strict approach is to prevent numerous applications and to maintain certainty in those situations.

Costs

In *Piglowska v Piglowska* [1999], the House of Lords drew attention to the principle of proportionality between legal costs incurred and the assets available. It was felt that there had been too many hearings in this case and that, in future, consideration had to be given to such matters. Despite the warning on costs, it would appear that high costs are still being incurred in fighting ancillary relief cases. In *L v L* [2002], the wife's appeal against the original order was successful, but the Court of Appeal highlighted the fact that nearly £1m had been spent by the parties in litigating.

FINANCIAL PROVISION AND PROPERTY ADJUSTMENT FOR CHILDREN

The law is found in the Child Support Acts 1991 and 1995 (as amended by the Child Support, Pensions and Social Security Act 2000). Note that the following is based on the law as amended in 2000, which has been implemented for all new cases. However, where children fall outside the remit of the Child Support Acts, financial provision and property adjustment orders are available under the MCA 1973. The criteria are contained in s 25(3), which closely follows the criteria for adults.

Also, there is provision in s 15 and Sched 1 to the Children Act (CA) 1989 for financial relief for children. An application under the CA 1989 may be for periodical payments, lump sums, settlements and transfers of property (Sched 1 para 1). However, if the application is made in the Family Proceedings Court, only the monetary orders are available, not property orders.

THE CHILD SUPPORT ACTS

The Child Support Acts set out to establish a mechanism for the assessment and enforcement of child maintenance, but only in respect of periodical payments. The Acts do not cover other forms of child support. The functions to be carried out under the Acts are the responsibility of the Child Support Agency. The family courts have no jurisdiction.

There will not now be an across-the-board transfer of cases from the original child maintenance ('old rules') system to the current system introduced by the reforms in 2003 ('current rules'). An old rules case will continue to be transferred to current rules if it becomes linked to a case dealt with under the current rules. Linked cases must be worked out under the same rules.

The Commission expects to introduce a new 'gross income' scheme in 2012. From that time, parents with existing 'old rules' or 'current rules' cases will be asked to choose whether they wish to apply to use the 'gross income' scheme or make a private arrangement with the other parent. This process is expected to take around three years.

Below is an outline of the changes made by the Child Maintenance & Other Payments Act 2008 and the 2003 system laid out below that, as both systems will run alongside each other until the revised scheme is implemented in 2012.

Child Maintenance & Other Payments Act 2008

Key changes introduced by the Act are:

1 There is no obligation for people on benefits to use the Child Maintenance and Enforcement Commission (CMEC).

2 The Child Support Agency no longer exists and has been replaced by the CMEC.

(a) The Commission will be under the power of the Secretary of State for Work and Pensions.

(b) The main object of the Commission is 'to maximise the number of those children who live apart from one or both of their parents for whom effective maintenance arrangements are in place' (s 2).

The Commission's main objective is supported by the following subsidiary objectives:

(a) to encourage and support the making and keeping by parents of appropriate voluntary maintenance arrangements for their children;

(b) to support the making of applications for child support maintenance under the Child Support Act 1991 (c 48) and to secure compliance when appropriate with parental obligations under that Act.

3 Changes to payments under s 16 Schedule 4

Part 1 of Schedule 1 to the Child Support Act 1991 (c 48): the weekly amount of child support maintenance payable is calculated by reference to the non-resident parent's net weekly income.

'Net' weekly income is replaced by 'gross' weekly income everywhere it occurs.

Change to basic rate

- 12% where the non-resident parent has one qualifying child;
- 16% where the non-resident parent has two qualifying children;
- 19% where the non-resident parent has three or more qualifying children.

THE CHILD SUPPORT AGENCY

This body was set up to deal with the maintenance of children by non-resident parents. Applications will be made to the Agency by the parent or person with care for the child for an order against the non-resident parent. Section 2 of the Child Support Act (CSA) 1991 states that the officers must have regard to the welfare of any child likely to be affected by decisions reached by use of their discretionary powers. However, the calculation of child support is subject to a strict straight line percentage deduction from income, and hence there is little scope for discretionary decisions.

TO WHOM DOES THE LEGISLATION APPLY?

The Acts only relate to those families falling within the definitions set out thus: there must be a qualifying child, a person with care and a non-resident parent.

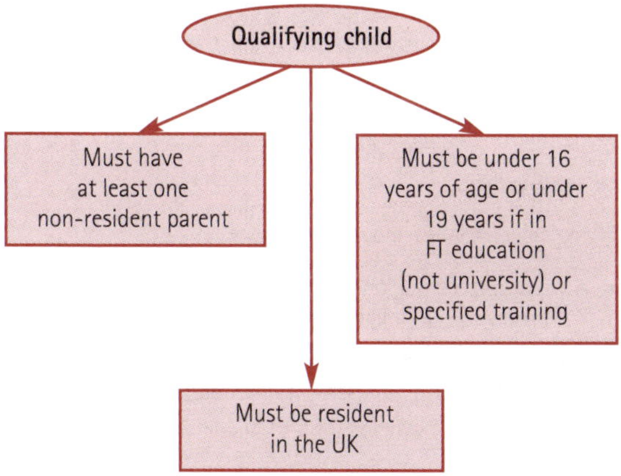

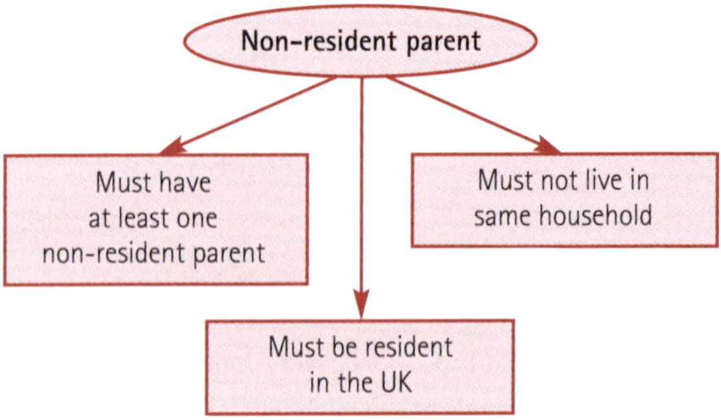

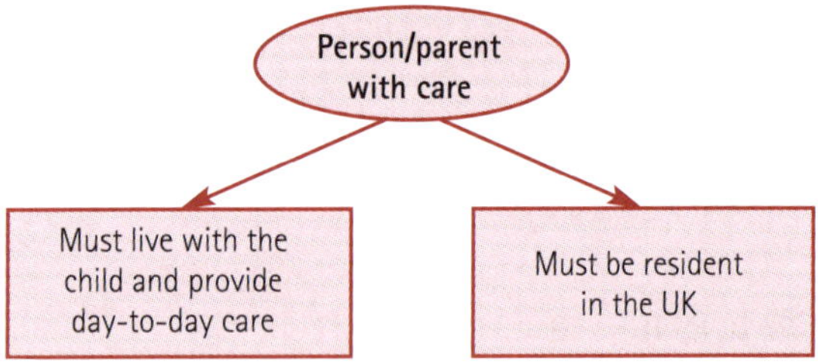

USING THE ACTS

Not all persons or parents with care are required to use the Agency and Acts as a means of child support calculation. Clearly, if the definitions are not applicable, there is no jurisdiction. If the Agency does have jurisdiction, then two scenarios apply:

Must use the Agency

- Qualifying child lives with a parent with care.
- Parent with care is receiving one of the specified welfare benefits (i.e. Income Support, income-related Job Seeker's Allowance, Disability Working Allowance) – the parent with care will be allowed to keep the first £10 of child support payable after assessment – the remainder 'pays back' the state for provision of welfare benefits for the child.

May use the Agency

- Qualifying child lives with a parent with care who is not claiming benefit.
- Qualifying child lives with person with care who may or may not be claiming benefit.
- Has a court order for child support (periodical payments) which was granted post-1993 and has been in existence for more than one year.

FAILURE TO COMPLY

If the parent with care falls into the first scenario and fails to comply with the Agency, the Agency will consider why this failure arises. If the parent with care can prove that compliance will result in violence or a threat of violence to themselves or the child, the Agency will treat non-compliance as justifiable. If the parent with care cannot prove this to the satisfaction of the Agency, the benefits payable to the parent with care will be reduced by up to 40 per cent.

ASSESSING THE CHILD SUPPORT PAYABLE

Only the non-resident parent (NRP) will be assessed in relation to their net income, and a variety of rates apply:

- a basic rate;
- a reduced rate;
- a flat rate; and
- a nil rate.

The basic rate is the following percentage of the NRP's net weekly income:

- 15 per cent for one qualifying child;
- 20 per cent for two qualifying children; and
- 25 per cent for three or more qualifying children.

This will apply where the net weekly income is above £200, subject to a cap, whereby income over £2,000 per week will be ignored.

The reduced rate will apply when the net weekly income is below £200 but above £100 per week. Payments will be on a sliding scale according to the income level, but will not be less than £7.00 per week.

The flat rate of £7.00 per week is payable by NRPs whose net income is below £100 per week, who receive prescribed benefits, pensions or allowances, or whose partners receive prescribed benefits.

The nil rate applies if the NRP is of a prescribed description or has a weekly income of less than £7.00.

Where the NRP has a second, resident family, the net income will be calculated differently. The net income for the purposes of child support will be reduced by the relevant percentage applicable for the number of resident children – i.e. if there is one resident child, the net income for the purposes of child support is total net income less 15 per cent.

VARIATIONS TO CHILD SUPPORT

If the NRP has high costs relating to seeing the qualifying child, or in relation to employment, or has made a large capital transfer, pre-1993, to the parent with care with the intention of reducing child support, an application to reduce the basic amount payable can be made. These adjustments are known as departures, and in reality do not result in any major reduction in child support payable.

ENFORCEMENT OF CHILD SUPPORT

The enforcement regime has been tightened up with regard to co-operation and payment of child support. Non-resident parents are now subject to a range of sanctions for non-compliance with the assessment process or payment:

- penalties of up to 25 per cent for late/non-payment of support payments;
- deductions from earnings orders;
- liability orders for non-payment which may be enforced by distress;
- commitment to prison;
- disqualification from driving.

However, the State owes no duty of care towards the individual to collect and enforce child maintenance. To impose such a duty would be to open the flood-gates. The correct remedy would be a judicial review of the State's failure in this regard: *R (Rowley) v SS for Work and Pensions* [2007] EWCA Civ 598.

THE COURT'S ROLE

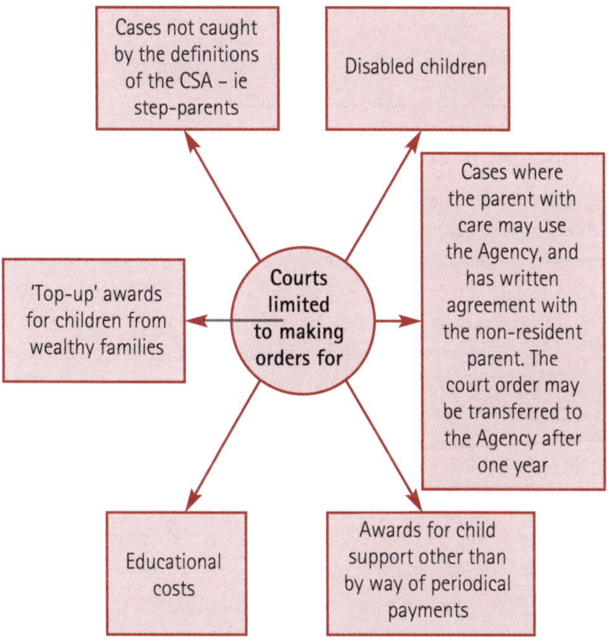

The legislation used to enable the court to make an order (see figure above), and to assess what support is reasonable, will, depending on the status of the applicant and the respondent, be:

- the Matrimonial Causes Act 1973;
- the Domestic Proceedings and Magistrates' Courts Act 1978; or
- the Children Act 1989.

The 1973 and 1989 Acts are most commonly used;

The type of order that can be granted may include:	The criteria to be applied depend on the Act used, but all focus on:
■ periodical payments; ■ lump sum orders; ■ property transfer orders.	■ income, earning capacity and financial resources; ■ financial needs, obligations and responsibilities; ■ financial needs of the child; ■ physical or mental disability of child; ■ expectations as to education of child.

CONTINUING REFORM

In the Green Paper, 'Strengthening Families, Promoting Parental Responsibility; The future of child maintenance' published in January 2011, proposals are made for complete reform of the child maintenance scheme. It is hoped these proposals will start to take effect in phases from 2012. The main focus of the revised scheme is to encourage families to make their own mutual agreements with regard to child support, which in turn will lead to less reliance on the government run collection scheme which has proved costly to the tax payer. The key proposals involve offering several new services:

- A gateway system to provide advice and to support separating families in making financial provision for their children.
- A package of support based on info provided by HM Revenue and Customs to enable families to make calculations and put in place their own arrangements.
- Charges for accessing statutory child maintenance, which will vary according to means and services opted for.

You should now be confident that you would be able to tick all of the boxes on the checklist at the beginning of this chapter. To check your knowledge of Financial remedies and orders on divorce why not visit the companion website and take the Multiple Choice Question test. Check your understanding of the terms and vocabulary used in this chapter with the flashcard glossary.

4

Family homes and domestic violence

PART IV OF THE FAMILY LAW ACT 1996

This deals with the reform of measures relating to the difficult area of domestic violence, which were previously contained in the Matrimonial Homes Act 1983, the Domestic Violence and Matrimonial Proceedings Act 1976 and the Domestic Proceedings and Magistrates' Courts Act 1978.

In *Richards v Richards* [1984], Scarman LJ described the situation as he saw it:

> The statutory provision is a hotchpotch of enactments of limited scope, passed into law to meet specific situations or to strengthen the powers of specified courts.

The aim of Part IV is to remove the complexity of the previous legislation, and to introduce a consistent range of remedies and criteria upon which they are based, throughout the courts that have jurisdiction in this area.

2 PRINCIPAL REMEDIES UNDER THE FLA 1996

1 Non-Molestation Order

2 Occupation Order

NON-MOLESTATION ORDERS (s 42)

A non-molestation order is an order containing either or both of the following provisions:

- prohibiting a person (the respondent) from molesting another person who is associated with the respondent;
- prohibiting the respondent from molesting a relevant child.

The definitions of 'relevant child' and 'associated' are contained in s 62(2) and (3)–(5). The class of possible applicants for non-molestation orders has been significantly widened to provide greater protection in cases of domestic violence.

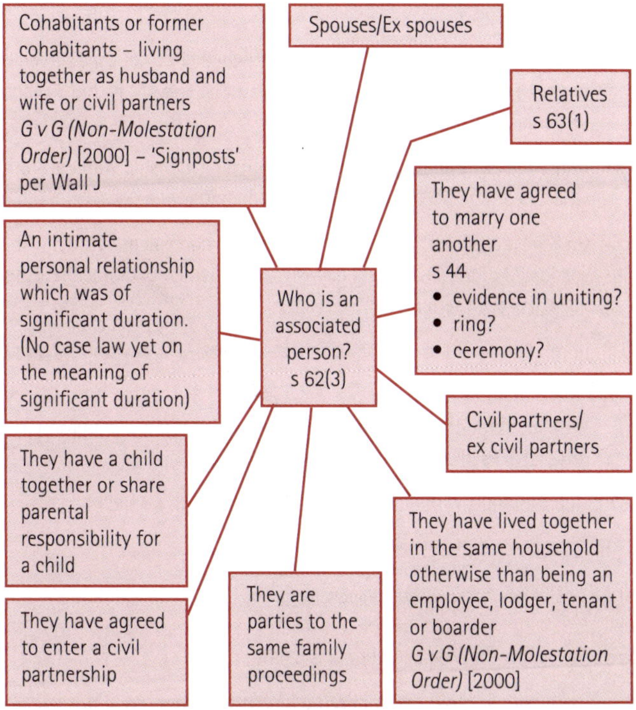

To apply for a non-molestation order the applicant and respondent must be associated, defined in s 62(3) and 62(4) FLA (as amended):

s 62(3):

For the purposes of this Part, a person is associated with another person if–

(a) they are or have been married to each other;

(aa) they are or have been civil partners of each other;

(b) they are cohabitants or former cohabitants;

(c) they live or have lived in the same household, otherwise than merely by reason of one of them being the other's employee, tenant, lodger or boarder;

(d) they are relatives;

(e) they have agreed to marry one another (whether or not that agreement has been terminated) – but application must be brought within 3 years of termination: s 44;

(ea) they have or have had an intimate personal relationship with each other which is or was of significant duration;

(eza) they have entered into a civil partnership agreement (as defined by section 73 of the Civil Partnership Act 2004) (whether or not that agreement has been terminated);

(f) in relation to any child, they are both persons falling within subsection (4); or

(g) they are parties to the same family proceedings (other than proceedings under this Part).

s 62(4) A person falls within this subsection in relation to a child if–

(a) he is a parent of the child; or

(b) he has or has had parental responsibility for the child.

A 'relative' is given a wide definition in s 63(1).

G v G (Non-Molestation Order: Jurisdiction) [2000] 2 FLR 533

The parties did not strictly speaking live together, but spent 4 or 5 nights per week together. The man said the parties had discussed marriage and he had sold his house and put the proceeds into a joint account from which he had spent money on the 'soon to be matrimonial home'. The woman was refused a non-molestation order by magistrates on the basis that she and the man were not associated persons within section 62, therefore they had no jurisdiction over the case. On appeal the woman admitted that the reason she said the parties did not live together was in order to preserve her state benefits. The Court held that on the question of jurisdiction, the evidence as a whole was sufficient to support the proposition that the parties were cohabitants. Wall J cited a supplementary benefits case, *Crake v SBC* [1982] 1 All ER 498, where certain 'signposts' were suggested to assist the court in coming to a decision as to whether parties were living together. These are:

(i) whether they are members of the same household;
(ii) if the relationship is stable;
(iii) if there is financial support;
(iv) if there is a sexual relationship;
(v) if they have children;
(vi) if there is public acknowledgement of the relationship.

Finally, Wall J stated that where domestic violence is concerned the Act should be given a purposive construction. So, jurisdiction should not be refused unless the facts of the case are plainly incapable of being brought within the statute.

Applications

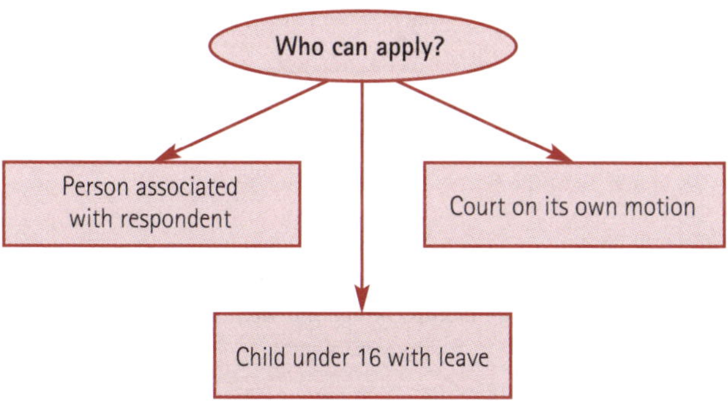

The court can make a non-molestation order:

- on an application made by *a person associated* with the respondent (with or without other family proceedings); or

- if, in any family proceedings to which the respondent is a party, the court considers that the order should be made for the benefit of the other party to the proceedings or any relevant child, even though no application has been made.

A child under the age of 16 cannot make an application for a non-molestation order without the leave of the court. The court may grant leave only if it considers that the child has sufficient understanding to make the application for a non-molestation order (s 43).

'Family proceedings' are defined as proceedings under the inherent jurisdiction of the High Court in relation to children and the following enactments:

(a) Parts I, II and IV of this Act;

(b) the MCA 1973;

(ba) Schedule 5 to the Civil Partnership Act 2004;

(d) the Adoption and Children Act 2002;

(e) the Domestic Proceedings and Magistrates' Courts Act 1978;

(ea) Schedule 6 to the Civil Partnership Act 2004;

(g) Part III of the Matrimonial and Family Proceedings Act 1984;

(h) the Family Law Act 1996;

(h) ss 11 and 12 of the Crime and Disorder Act 1998.

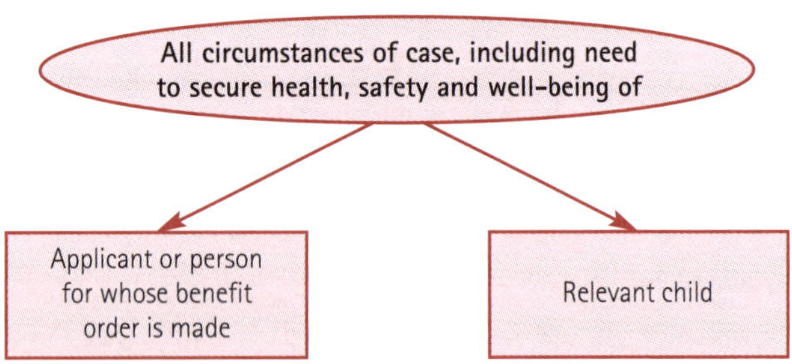

The court will consider all the circumstances including the need to secure the health, safety and well-being of the applicant and/or relevant child. The focus is on the need for protection in the future, not what has happened in the past.

Well-being includes any psychological effects – *R v Ireland* [1997].

What is molestation?

Molestation is not defined in the Act. Section 42(6) as to the scope of an order is left wide and therefore a non-molestation order can be made to cover either particular or general molestation and can be made for a specified period or until further order. Examples of behaviour considered to be molestation can be seen in the following cases:

- *Horner v Horner* [1982]: the husband handed the wife upsetting notes and intercepted her on her way to the station.
- *Johnson v Walton* [1990]: the husband sent embarrassing photographs of his wife to a local newspaper with intent to cause her distress. The court said that molestation can include *any* behaviour intended to cause distress or harm.

Intentional conduct?

Whether or not the conduct is unintentional does not prevent the court from making an order. Concentration must be on the effect of the respondent's conduct on the applicant or relevant child: *G v G (Occupation Order: Conduct)* [2000] 2 FLR 36.

If the order is made within family proceedings, it will cease to have effect when those proceedings are withdrawn or dismissed. Non-molestation orders, traditionally, were not granted for a lengthy period, being seen as first aid rather than major surgery. The FLA simply states that the order may be made 'until further order', leaving the duration to the discretion of the court (*M v W (Non-Molestation Order: Duration)* [2000]). Orders may be varied or discharged by the court by application of the original applicant, or the respondent. In addition the court can vary or discharge the order on its own motion.

G v G (Occupation Order: Conduct) [2000] 2 FLR 36

The wife applied for an occupation order for her and the children to remain in the home and oust the husband. The trial judge found significant harm but that it was not attributable to the husband as it was unintentional. The Court of Appeal held that the court's concentration must be on the effect of conduct, rather than the party's intention. Thus whether conduct is intentional/unintentional is not the issue. An applicant is entitled to protection from unjustifiable conduct that causes harm to her or the children.

Additionally, the court is free to consider regulation of the matrimonial home when refusing to make an ouster order. The husband was ordered to leave the main bedroom, leaving it for the wife alone.

Ex parte applications for non-molestation orders

As the need for protection from violence can arise in emergencies, there may be a need for orders without notice, and the court has the power under s 45 to grant such orders. Non-molestation orders can be granted without notice to the respondent if the court considers that it is just and convenient to do so. (This power is also available for occupation orders but very rarely used in this situation.)

When deciding these matters, the court will consider all the circumstances, including:

- s 45(2)(a) FLA 1996 any risk of significant harm to the applicant or a relevant child attributable to the conduct of the respondent if an order is not made immediately; and
- s 45(2)(b) FLA 1996 whether it is likely that the applicant will be deterred or prevented from pursuing the application if an order is not made immediately; and
- s 45(2)(c) FLA 1996 whether there is reason to believe that the respondent is aware of the proceedings but is deliberately evading service and the applicant or a relevant child will be seriously prejudiced by the delay involved:

- where the court is a magistrates' court, in effecting service of proceedings; or
- in any other case, in effecting substituted service.

BREACH OF ARTICLE 6?

The court must allow the respondent an opportunity to make representations at a full hearing as soon as it is just and convenient to do so; therefore there is no breach of Article 6, the right to a fair hearing. *Re J (Abduction: Rights of Custody* [2000]).

RIGHTS TO OCCUPY MATRIMONIAL HOME (S 30)

Section 30(1) gives the non-estate holding spouse the right to occupy the matrimonial home if the other spouse is entitled to occupy by virtue of a beneficial estate or interest, a contract or any enactment.

These 'home rights' (HRs) are:

- if in occupation, a right not to be evicted or excluded from the dwelling house or any part of it by the other spouse, except with the leave of the court given by a s 33 order;
- if not in occupation, a right (with the leave of the court) to enter into and occupy the dwelling house.

Section 31 states that HRs are charges on the estate or interest of the other spouse and have the same priority as if an equitable interest has been created on one of the following dates, whichever is the latest:

- the date on which the spouse so entitled acquires the estate or interest;
- the date of the marriage; or
- 1 January 1968 (the commencement date of the Matrimonial Homes Act 1967).

Even though MHRs are charges, these rights are brought to an end by the death of the other spouse or upon termination of the marriage (other than by death), unless an order exists under s 33(5). The charge takes priority after an existing mortgage.

Occupation orders

Where a person is entitled to occupy a dwelling house by virtue of a beneficial estate, interest, contract or MHR in relation to a dwelling house, and that dwelling house is, has been or was intended to be the home of that person or another person associated with him, then he can apply for an occupation order. Where an agreement to marry is terminated, that person can also apply for such an order, but the application must be made within three years of the termination of the agreement. The time runs from the day that the agreement to marry ends.

The range of permitted applicants is narrower than for non-molestation orders and applicants are split into two categories – *'entitled'* and *'non-entitled'*. Section 62(1) defines cohabitants as 'a man and woman who, although not married to each other, are living together as husband and wife'. Since the enactment of the Civil Partnership Act 2004 the statute has been updated to include cohabitants living together as civil partners (s 62(1)).

> Available if respondent has used/threatened to use violence against applicant/relevant child.
>
> Power attached unless adequate protection without the power.
>
> If no power of arrest attached and applicant considers that respondent has failed to comply with order, applicant can seek warrant.

Occupation orders under s 33 – Entitled applicants

Entitled applicants can seek an occupation order as against any associated person (see flowchart on page 70).

Guiding principles:

- An order overriding proprietary interests is draconian: *Chalmers v Johns* [1999].
- Occupation orders are only justified in exceptional circumstances: *Chalmers v Johns* [1999].
- The availability of alternative housing does not oblige the court to make an order: *Re Y* (Children) Occupation Order [2000]; *B v B (Occupation Order)* [1999].

- The court can refuse to make an ouster order and in the alternative regulate boundaries for occupation within the family home: *G v G (Occupation Order: Conduct)* [2000].

CHALMERS V JOHNS [1999] 1 FLR 392

An occupation order is draconian. It is an order that overrides proprietary rights and is therefore an order that is only justified in exceptional circumstances. The Court of Appeal gave guidance to approaching the statute:

- section 33(6) applies in less severe cases and provides a discretionary remedy, but section 33(7) applies in serious cases. The court should look to section 33(7) first to consider whether it is compelled to make an order. If the balance of harm test is not satisfied the court should then go on to consider the section 33(6) checklist and whether it should exercise its discretion to make an order.

RE Y (Children) (Occupation Order) [2000] 2 FCR 470

There was hatred in the house and fighting, principally between the father and his pregnant 16-year-old daughter. The mother sided with the daughter and the 13-year-old son with his father. Both the mother and father made cross-applications for ouster orders. Both parties would have been a priority for local authority housing.

The court considered that the mother was at least no worse than the father and was not satisfied that there was significant harm. Despite the parties being local housing priorities the Court of Appeal refused to make an ouster order.

B v B (Occupation Order) [1999] 1 FLR 715

The wife had been forced out of the house by the husband's violence, taking their baby with her. The husband remained in the home with a six-year-old boy, who was his son by a previous relationship. The husband appealed against an order ousting him, on the basis that it would cause the boy significant harm. The Court of Appeal focused attention on section 33(6), the housing needs and resources of the parties. Whereas the local housing authority had a duty to re-house the wife in suitable permanent accommodation, their duty to the husband was lower because if he were to be ousted he would be rendered 'intentionally homeless'. Additionally the Court considered the boy's need to stay at the local school and found that, although the wife and baby were likely to suffer significant harm which was attributable to the husband's conduct, the effect on the son as a relevant child would be such that he would suffer greater harm if the order were made.

Effect of the order

The s 33(3) order may:

- enforce the applicant's entitlement to remain in occupation as against the other person (the respondent);
- require the respondent to permit the applicant to enter and remain in the dwelling house or part of it;
- regulate the occupation of the dwelling house by either or both parties;
- if the respondent is entitled by virtue of a beneficial estate or interest or contract, prohibit, suspend or restrict the exercise of his right to occupy the dwelling house;
- if the respondent has MHRs in relation to the dwelling house and the applicant is the other spouse, restrict or terminate those rights;
- require the respondent to leave the dwelling house or part of it; or
- exclude the respondent from a defined area in which the dwelling house is included.

The important measure here is the power to exclude the respondent from a defined area.

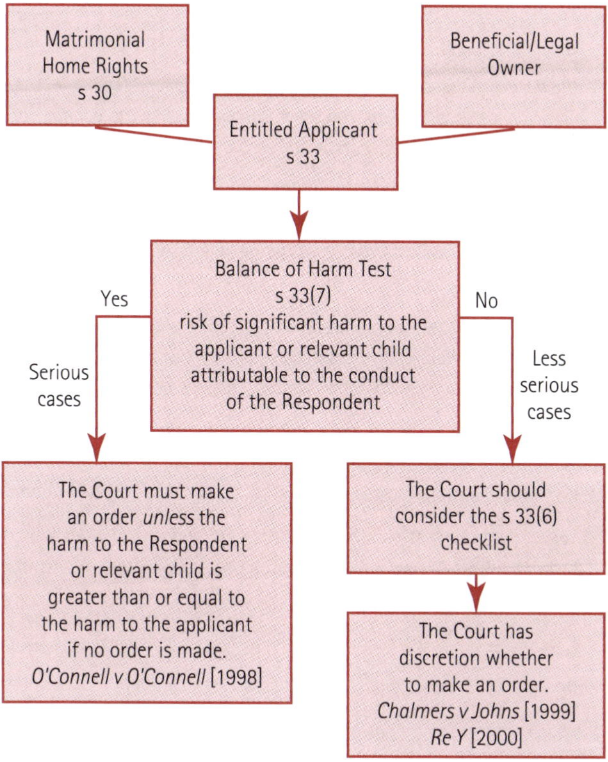

Applicant entitled to occupy – will use s 33

The home must have been or intended to be the home of the applicant and a person with whom she is associated: s 33(1) (b) and that person will be the respondent to the application.

The legal test: (as explained in Chalmers v Johns [1999] 1 FLR 392 (CA))

The court will first apply the 'balance of harm' test: s 33(7):

*If it appears to the court that the applicant or any relevant child is likely to suffer significant harm attributable to the conduct of the respondent if an order under this section . . . is **not** made the court **shall** make the order **unless** it appears to it that:*

(a) the respondent or any relevant child is likely to suffer significant harm if the order is made; and

(b) the harm likely to be suffered by the respondent or child in that event is as great as, or greater than, the harm attributable to the conduct of the respondent which is likely to be suffered by the applicant or child if the order is not made.

So the first question is whether it is likely that the applicant or any relevant child will suffer significant harm due to the behaviour of the respondent if an order is not made?

If No, then the significant harm test is not satisfied and does not apply. The court retains a discretion whether or not to make an occupation order, and will exercise that discretion in accordance with s 33(6) (see below).

If Yes, the court must make the order unless any significant harm likely to be suffered by the respondent /relevant child if the order is made is at least as great as the harm suffered by the applicant/relevant child if order is not made.

If the respondent/relevant child would suffer as much harm then the court nevertheless retains a discretion to make the occupation order in accordance with s 33(6).

The discretionary exercise under s 33(6)

The court must have regard to all the circumstances including:

(a) the housing needs and housing resources of each of the parties and of any relevant child;

(b) the financial resources of each of the parties;

(c) the likely effect of any order, or of any decision by the court not to

[make an order] on the health, safety or well-being of the parties, and of any relevant child; and

(d) the conduct of the parties in relation to each other and otherwise.

G v G [2000] (CA):

Parties were divorcing. W said H's behaviour at home, although not violent, was causing great tension and strain on W and children. At first instance Judge refused to make occupation order on ground that as H's conduct was unintentional, it could not be said that likelihood of harm could be attributed to him under s 33(7).

On appeal CA held important factor under s 33(7) was not the intention of the respondent, but the effect of his conduct. Nonetheless, on the facts, an order regulating the use of the home was sufficient, and an exclusion order was not justified.

Obligations that courts may apply to occupation orders

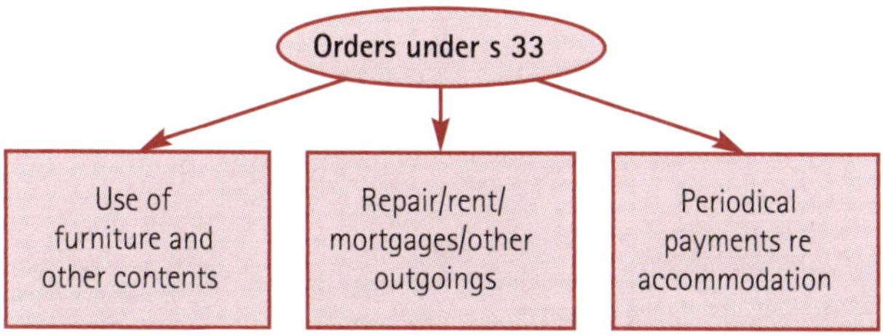

However, *Ngowbe v Ngowbe* [2000] exposed a fatal flaw in enforcing such orders. The Act has yet to be amended to rectify this.

Duration of order

Under s 33, the court may make an order for a specified period (often quite short) or until a further order is made. If the applicant for the order is seeking it due to their MHRs (and hence the application is made during the subsistence of the marriage), the court can state that the order shall not end due to the death of the other party, or due to the termination of the marriage (otherwise than by death).

Occupation orders under ss 35, 36, 37 and 38 – non-entitled applicants

Occupation orders under these sections will refer to applicants and respondents within the specified status for each section. Non-entitled applicants cannot apply for an order against any associated person. The criteria and effects of the orders are all similar to those for s 33 above, but with slight changes as highlighted below. The maximum duration of the order is specific to the individual section.

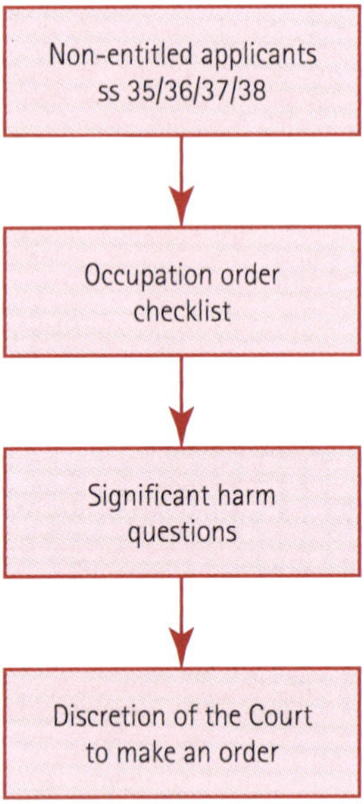

Section 35

- Applicant is a former spouse with no right to occupy the home.
- Criteria as for s 33, but with three extra factors:
  - The length of time that has elapsed since the parties lived together.
  - The length of time that has elapsed since the marriage was brought to an end.
  - The existence of any pending proceedings relating to the property by way of an application for a property adjustment order, declaration of legal/beneficial ownership or an application under the CA 1989 for a property adjustment order.
- Duration: specified duration of up to six months with extension possible by application on one or more occasions for no longer than six months per application.

Section 36

- Applicant is a cohabitant or former cohabitant with no existing right to occupy. See definition of cohabitant (s 62(1)).
- The balance of significant harm test becomes the balance of harm questions as there is no obligation upon the court to make an order where significant harm is made out.

  In addition, the checklist takes account of the following extra factors:

  - The nature of the parties' relationship.
  - The length of time that they have lived as husband and wife.
  - Whether there are, or have been, any children of the parties or for whom they have/had parental responsibility.
  - The length of time that has elapsed since the parties lived together.
  - The existence of any pending proceedings relating to the property by way of a declaration of legal/beneficial ownership or an application under the CA 1989 for a property adjustment order.
- Duration: specified duration of up to six months with extension possible by application on one more occasion for no longer than six months (s 36(10)).

Section 37

- Applicant is a spouse or former spouse and neither party has a right to occupy.
- Criteria as for s 33.
- Duration: specified duration of up to six months with extension possible by application on one or more occasions for no longer than six months per application.

Section 38

- Applicant is a cohabitant or former cohabitant and neither party has a right to occupy.
- Criteria as s 36.
- Duration: specified duration of up to six months with extension possible by application on one more occasion for no longer than six months.

Transfer of tenancies

Another aspect of what arguably could be seen as protection, furthered by the Act in Sched 7, is the ability of the courts to transfer certain types of tenancies on divorce or separation of cohabitants.

The types of tenancies which are included are:

- a protected tenancy or statutory tenancy within the meaning of the Rent Act 1977;
- a statutory tenancy within the meaning of the Rent (Agriculture) Act 1976;
- a secure tenancy within the meaning of s 79 of the Housing Act 1985; and
- an assured tenancy or assured agricultural occupancy within the meaning of Part I of the Housing Act 1988.

The power is available to the court when one spouse is entitled to occupy a dwelling house by virtue of a relevant tenancy, either in his own right or jointly with the other spouse. The court also has power to make a property adjustment order under s 23A (divorce or separation) or s 24 (nullity). Where there is entitlement, it is also available to cohabitants who cease to live together as husband and wife.

The dwelling house in question must have been the matrimonial home of the spouses or the home where the cohabitants lived as husband and wife.

In deciding this matter, the court shall have regard to all the circumstances of the case, including:

- the circumstances in which the tenancy was granted to either or both parties or the circumstances in which they became tenants under the tenancy;
- the matters mentioned in s 36(6)(a)–(c) (needs and resources and considerations with respect to children) and, where the parties are cohabitants and only one of them is entitled to occupy the dwelling house by virtue of the relevant tenancy, the further matters mentioned in s 36(6)(e)–(h) (nature and length of relationship, children for whom they have had parental responsibility and how long they have lived apart); and
- the suitability of the parties as tenants. The court should also give the landlord of the dwelling house an opportunity to be heard.

Under s 53 and Part II of Sched 7, the court can transfer a tenancy from one party to the other or, if it is a joint tenancy, to one party alone. All the privileges, obligations, liabilities and any indemnities will be transferred along with the tenancy.

Under Part III, the court may order the transferee to pay compensation to the transferor, but may defer such payment or allow payment by instalments. When deciding these matters, the court will consider all the circumstances, as well as:

- the financial loss to the transferor that would otherwise occur as a result of the order;
- the financial needs and resources of the parties;
- the financial obligations that the parties have or are likely to have in the foreseeable future, including such obligations to each other and any children.

However, the ability to defer or allow instalments will only be available if to order immediate payment would cause the transferee greater financial hardship than that which would be suffered by the transferor if it was granted.

Even if the tenancy is transferred, the court may order that both parties should be jointly and severally liable for the discharge or performance of all obligations and liabilities in respect of the dwelling house which previously fell to only one of the parties. If such an order is made, the court may also direct that an indemnity by one party to the other be made for carrying out the obligations.

The appropriate time for transfers taking effect is, in the case of nullity, on the granting of the decree absolute and, in the case of divorce or separation, the date to be determined as if the court was making a property adjustment under s 23A of the Matrimonial Causes Act (MCA) 1973.

No application for a transfer can be made by a spouse after the remarriage of that spouse.

POWERS OF ARREST

Under s 47, the court, on making an occupation order, where it appears that the respondent has used or threatened violence against the applicant or relevant child, shall attach a power of arrest to one or more of the provisions of the order unless it is satisfied that the applicant or child will be adequately protected without such a power. Thus, there is a presumption that there will be a power of arrest attached.

This does not apply to orders without notice, but the court can attach a power of arrest if it is satisfied that the respondent has used or threatened violence against the applicant or relevant child and there is a risk of significant harm to the applicant or relevant child, attributable to the conduct of the respondent, if the power of arrest is not attached to the provisions immediately.

If the power of arrest is attached, then a constable may arrest without warrant a person whom he has reasonable cause for suspecting to be in breach of any such provision. A person who is arrested must be brought before the relevant judicial authority within 24 hours and, if the matter is not disposed of then, he may be remanded.

If the court has made an order but has not attached a power of arrest or has only attached the power to certain provisions of the order, then, if the applicant considers that the respondent has failed to comply with the order, he may apply to the court for the issue of a warrant for the arrest of the respondent. The court may only issue the warrant if it is satisfied that the application is substantiated on oath and has reasonable grounds for believing that the respondent has failed to comply with the order.

BREACH OF A NON-MOLESTATION ORDER – S 42A

Following the implementation of the Domestic Violence, Crime and Victims Act 2004 breach of a non-molestation order is now a criminal offence, therefore removing the need to attach a power of arrest to the order. Surprisingly, the same is not true of an occupation order, and hence powers of arrest will still be necessary here. If criminal proceedings are taken, enforcement of a non-molestation order cannot be done via the civil law (see *Lomas v Parle* [2003]).

Undertakings – s 46

In any case where the court can make occupation orders or non-molestation orders, the court may accept an undertaking from any party to the proceedings and no power of arrest can be attached to an undertaking. However, the court shall not accept an undertaking in any case where, apart from this restriction, a power of arrest would be attached.

AMENDMENTS TO THE CHILDREN ACT 1989

Important additions to the protective powers available to the courts have been introduced by amendments to Schedule 6 to the Children Act. Under s 38A of the Children Act, where the court is satisfied that the requirements for an interim care order have been met, the court may include an exclusion requirement if:

(a) there is reasonable cause to believe that, if a person (the relevant person) is excluded from a dwelling house in which the child lives, the child will cease to suffer or cease to be likely to suffer significant harm; and

(b) another person living in the dwelling house (whether a parent of the child or some other person):
- (i) is able and willing to give to the child the care which it would be reasonable to expect a parent to give him; and
- (ii) consents to the inclusion of the exclusion requirement.

The court has the power to attach the power of arrest to an exclusion requirement. A constable may arrest without warrant any person whom he has reasonable cause to believe to be in breach of the requirement.

If, while the interim care order with an exclusion requirement is in force, the local authority removes the child from the dwelling house from which the relevant person is excluded for a continuous period of more than 24 hours, the exclusion requirement of the order will cease to have effect. If the court accepts an undertaking in place of making an exclusion requirement, then no power of arrest can be attached.

Under s 44A of the Children Act 1989, the court now also has the ability to attach an exclusion requirement to an emergency protection order if it is satisfied that:

(a) there is reasonable cause to believe that if a person (the relevant person) is excluded from a dwelling house in which the child lives, then:
- (i) in the case of an order made on the ground mentioned in s 44(1)(a), the child will not be likely to suffer significant harm, even though the child is not removed as mentioned in s 44(1)(a)(i) or does not remain as mentioned in s 44(1)(a)(ii); or

(ii) in the case of an order made on the ground mentioned in para (b) or (c) of s 44(1), the inquiries referred to in that paragraph will cease to be frustrated; and

(b) another person living in the dwelling house (whether a parent of the child or some other person):
  (i) is able and willing to give to the child the care which it would be reasonable to expect a parent to give him; and
  (ii) consents to the inclusion of the exclusion requirement.

The factors to be considered when dealing with the power of arrest are the same as the case with the interim care order, as is the situation with undertakings. Also, the definition of an exclusion requirement is common to both sections:

(a) a provision requiring the relevant person to leave a dwelling house in which he is living with the child;

(b) a provision prohibiting the relevant person from entering a dwelling house in which the child lives;

(c) a provision excluding the relevant person from a defined area in which the dwelling house in which the child lives is situated.

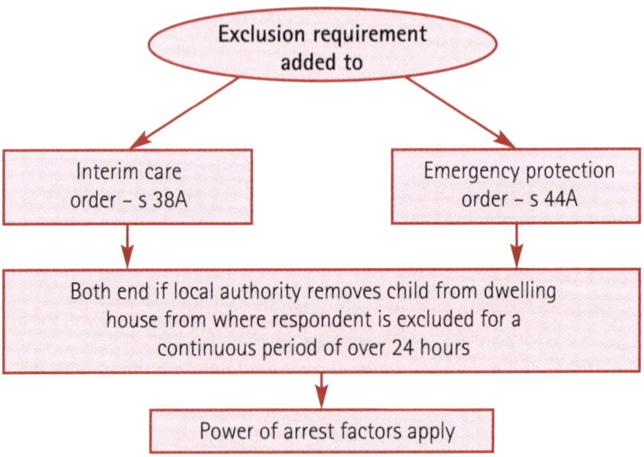

PROTECTION FROM HARASSMENT ACT 1997

Although Part IV of the FLA 1996 has increased the amount of protection available in cases of domestic violence for family members and other 'associated persons', there is still a need to protect those not covered by the FLA.

The main provisions of the Act are as follows.

Section 1(1)

A person must not pursue a course of conduct:

(a) which amounts to harassment of another; and

(b) which he knows or ought to know amounts to harassment of another.
- 'Course of conduct', at least two occasions: s 7(3).
- 'Harassment', includes speech: s 7(4).
- 'Knows/ought to know', objective test: s 1(2).

Section 1(3) contains exemptions if the person pursuing the conduct can show that:

- it was pursued for the purpose of preventing/detecting crime;
- it was pursued under any enactment or rule of law or to comply with any condition or requirement imposed by any person under any enactment; or
- in the particular circumstances, the pursuit of the course of conduct was reasonable.

The purpose of these exemptions is to allow certain occupations to be followed without the persons involved committing an offence, for example, investigative journalists, debt collectors, private investigators, etc. It is up to the persons claiming exemption to show that it applies.

CRIMINAL OFFENCES

Section 2

A person who breaches s 1 is guilty of harassment.

Summary conviction – six months and/or fine.

Section 4

Deals with putting people in fear of violence.

Section 4(1): course of conduct – at least two occasions – causes another to fear violence if he knows/ought to know that the conduct will cause the other to fear violence on those occasions. Again, an objective test: s 4(2).

Section 4(3) contains exemptions, as in s 1(3) above.

Summary conviction – six months and/or fine.

Conviction on indictment – five years and/or fine.

If the defendant is found not guilty of a s 4 offence, he may still be found guilty of a s 2 offence.

Section 5

Allows a court to impose a restraining order on a person convicted of a s 4 offence. The order will last for a specified period or until further order.

The order will prohibit:

- further harassment;
- putting people in fear of violence.

Breach of such an order:

Summary conviction – six months and/or fine.

Conviction on indictment – five years and/or fine.

The Domestic Violence, Crime and Victims Act 2004 has introduced a new s 5A into the act which enables the court to make a restraining order where the defendant has not even been convicted of an offence.

CIVIL REMEDIES

Section 3

Section 3(1): allows a civil claim for an actual or apprehended breach of s 1 by the victim of the course of conduct.

Section 3(2): court may award damages for, for example, anxiety caused by the harassment and any financial loss resulting from the harassment.

Section 3(3): the High Court/county court may grant injunctions restraining the defendant from pursuing harassing conduct, and, if the claimant considers that there has been a breach, he may apply for a warrant for the arrest of the defendant.

You should now be confident that you would be able to tick all of the boxes on the checklist at the beginning of this chapter. To check your knowledge of Family homes and domestic violence why not visit the companion website and take the Multiple Choice Question test. Check your understanding of the terms and vocabulary used in this chapter with the flashcard glossary.

5

Children I

The nature of the relationship between parents and their children, and the respective rights that they hold, is subject to change as societal views alter. Today there is an increasing recognition of children's individual rights, and the fact that these exist in parallel with, or to the exclusion of, parental rights. However, a child may not always be in a position to exercise rights, perhaps due to their age, and so the law places duties on parents to do so. The state of flux that exists between the extent of parents' rights vis à vis children's rights is illustrated in the case of *Gillick v West Norfolk AHA* [1986]. This case introduced the concept of the *Gillick* competent child, one who was of sufficient age and understanding to take decisions for themselves, rather than this resting with the parents. Although the extent of *Gillick* in terms of reducing the role for parents may be overstated, the case has informed the major piece of legislation relating to children, the Children Act 1989. This Act does not however set out in detail the nature of parents' duties in relation to their children, these are established in case law.

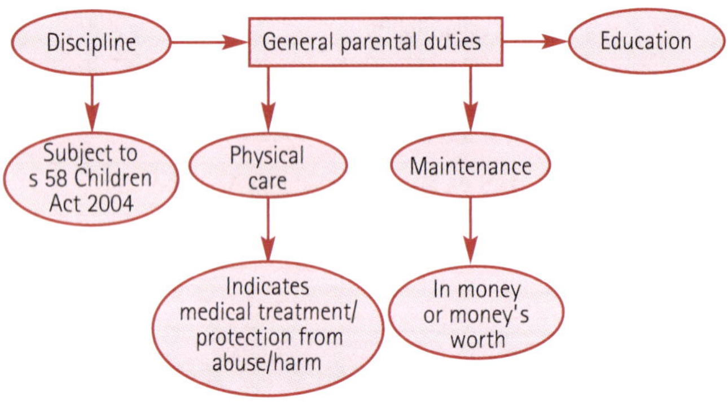

Academics and the courts submit that the law governing parental responsibility laid down in the Children Act 1989 refers to parental interests in children and not rights. So that the preferred application of the principle 'responsibilities' and not rights reflects the concept that children are owed duties rather than 'rights' granted to the parents in respect of or over their children. In the House of Lords, Lord Scarman argued that 'parental rights are derived from parental duty and exist only so long as they are needed for the protection of person and property of the child.' *Gillick v W Norfolk and Wisbech AHA* [1986]. Bainham suggests the position is not straightforward and suggests that parents have rights because they have responsibilities and they have responsibilities because they have rights. Bridgeman considers that rights flow from the parent child relationship.

Being a parent in law

Bainham (1999) states the law distinguishes between the following (which increases the flexibility within the law):

- Parentage – those who are genetically related to the child – man who provided the sperm and woman who provided the egg, combined to make a foetus, then a child.
- Parenthood – those regarded as parents in law, usually those who have parentage but not necessarily so. A man donating sperm is not always considered as the father. For example section 41 Human Fertilisation and Embryology Act 2008 makes it clear a man donating sperm to a clinic is not the father of a child if the sperm is used according to the donor's consent.
- Parental responsibility – those who have legal responsibility and 'rights'/obligations/interests attached to being a parent.

In addition there are various provisions in law that uphold the rights, responsibilities and duties of parents despite the fact the word parent is not defined in the Children Act 1989. These can be found in:

- Article 5 United Nations Convention on the Rights of the Child 1989 states 'Parties shall respect the responsibilities, rights and duties of parents.'
- Article 18(1) United Nations Convention on the rights of the Child 1989 states 'parties shall use their best efforts to ensure recognition of the principle that both parents have common responsibilities for the upbringing and development of the child, and that parents or guardians have the primary responsibility for the upbringing and development of the child.'
- Human Rights Act 1998 – implications for both parents and children.

In *Re G (Residence: Same Sex Partner)* [2006] Hale states parents can be classified as legal and or natural parents and that a person can become a natural parent in one of three ways:

- Genetic parenthood – where the parent provides the gametes which produce the child.

- Gestational parenthood – where the parent conceives and bears the child.
- Social and psychological parenthood – is the person that undertakes the day-to-day care and nurturing of the child.

Hale states that mostly mothers would combine all three types of natural parenthood and the father would combine two. A legal parent is the parent who is regarded as the parent of a child in the eyes of the law.

Who is a parent?

It is important to know who a parent of a child is for a variety of reasons. For example to enable a father to make an application for an order under the Children Act 1989 for contact, parental responsibility or a residence order. Alternatively a mother may need to know the paternity of her child to claim child support, amend a birth certificate or for inheritance rights or obtaining citizenship. In addition the bond between children and their parents can amount to family life under Article 8 Human Rights Act 1998 and the courts must do their best to foster co-operation between parents and maintain the bond between parent and child (*Kosmoplou v Greece* (Application No 60457/00) [2004]), particularly in applications made for contact and residence.

Establishing parentage

Who is the child's mother?

The woman who gives birth to a child is the mother of that child and this is affirmed in Ampthill Peerage Case [1977]. It is a well-established principle that the genetic link is irrelevant in establishing legal motherhood. For example where assisted reproduction has occurred. Section 33(1) Human Fertilisation and Embryology Act 2008 reflects this and states:

'The woman who is carrying or has carried a child as a result of the placing in her of an embryo or of sperm and eggs, and no other woman, is to be treated as the mother of the child.'

This is supported by the commentary in *Re G (Residence: Same Sex Partner)* [2006], which affirms that in relation to motherhood, it is the gestational link that is crucial and that this is established by the closeness of the bond through pregnancy and the pain and effort of bearing a child (para 34).

The current law is clear in that only the woman that gives birth to the child is the mother. In same sex couple relationships, the second mother will be classed if in a civil partnership at the time of the birth, as the 'second female partner' under section 42 Human Fertilisation and Embryology Act 2008.

A woman can also become the mother of a child if an adoption order or parental order is made in her favour.

Who is the child's father?

If a child is born to a married couple it is presumed that the husband is the father of the child under the *pater est* presumption. Although questions about the relevance of this presumption were raised in *Re H and A (Children)* [2002] as more children are born out of marriage and science has developed to allow DNA testing, which avoids the need to use presumptions to prove paternity.

If the father is not married to the child's mother he does not currently have the right to have his name entered on to the birth certificate to reflect that he is the child's father, unless the mother consents. The law is currently under review in this area and plans to amend the law are likely under the Welfare Reform Act 2010 that has been put in place.

If fatherhood is disputed a scientific test can be directed by the courts but the court will consider the child's rights and interests to know their true identity. This issue is illustrated in case law and demonstrates the balance that needs to be weighed in terms of what is considered to be in the best interests of the child.

Under the Births and Deaths Registration Act 1953 s 43(2), the law presumes that a man will be the child's father if his name is on the birth certificate of a child. There is a statutory obligation that requires the birth to be registered within 42 days.

A man can also become the father of a child if an adoption order or parental order is made in his favour.

Parenthood – Assisted Reproduction

Primarily governed by two acts, the Human Fertilisation and Embryology Acts 1990 and 2008. Part 2 of the 2008 HFEA makes changes to the law governing parenthood & assisted reproduction. The rules were extended on parenthood to include lesbian couples, whether or not they are civil partners. The new provisions only apply to treatment received after April 2009 and are not retrospective.

Who is the child's mother?

The woman who is carrying or has carried a child as a result of the placing in her an embryo or of sperm and eggs – no other woman is treated as the mother of the child HFEA 2008 s 33(1), regardless of where conception occurred.

Who is the child's father?

- Married couples – a husband will automatically be the legal father unless he did not consent under HFEA 2008 s 35(1) regardless of where conception occurred. Although note the outcome of *Leeds Teaching Hospital NHS Trust v A* [2003] where there was a mix up in the sperm used. In this case A (husband of wife) was found not to have consented to the placing of that embryo, using the sperm from B (another donor) and he was also found not to have consented to the treatment, which used the sperm from another. Hence he was not the father of the child. The genetic father was found to be B.
- Unmarried couples – where a woman has a child as a result of insemination in a UK licensed clinic and the couple have in place at the time of the transfer of the embryo, resulting in conception, an agreement that the man consents to being treated as the father, for any child resulting from the treatment – he is the legal parent HFEA 2008 ss 36 and 37.
- For lesbian couples in a civil partnership, that have a child conceived before April 2009, the non-birth mother has no automatic recognition as a parent and no automatic parental responsibility. This can only be acquired by agreement or court order.
- If a lesbian couple have a child that is conceived after April 2009, s 42 HFEA 2008 provides, where a female civil partner gives birth, a child born as a result of donor insemination, whether in the UK or elsewhere is the mother and her civil partner is automatically the other parent in law, unless that person did not consent to treatment. This is the same position as for married couples.
- Lesbian couples who are not civil partners HFEA 2008 ss 43 and 44. The law here is the same as for lesbian civil partners, EXCEPT that the mother's lesbian partner will be the parent in law ONLY if the child was conceived at a licensed clinic in the UK.

Surrogacy

By agreement, another woman can agree to bear a child for a couple. In these circumstances an agreement can be drawn up to reflect the intention of the parties. It is usual that the surrogate mother agrees to hand over the child to those defined in the agreement and waives any right to exercise parental responsibility for payment of reasonable expenses. In a surrogacy arrangement the gestational mother and genetic father are the legal parents.

However the parents that enter into a surrogacy agreement can, in accordance with section 54 HFEA 2008 apply for a parenting order following a surrogacy arrangement which will enable them to have the legal status of parents. This section applies to married couples, those in a civil partnership, or those in an enduring relationship. In accordance with section 54(3) HFEA 2008, an application must be made within six months of the child's birth. The conditions that must be fulfilled are strict. If there is a dispute between the surrogate mother and parents, the court will use the welfare principle to determine what is in the best interests of the child with regard to residence.

THE CHILDREN ACT 1989

The Children Act 1989 introduced a variety of new principles into the operation of the law in family relationships. It emphasises the importance of the child's welfare, how the child's needs should be met, the extent to which the state (whether the court or a local authority) can intervene, and establishes key concepts, such as parental responsibility.

An important aim of the Act is to provide a flexible, consistent set of remedies and orders which will be available at all levels of the legal system and to make them available whether the matter is one of private or public law. This attempt at unification of both areas of law has been largely successful and has provided much sought-after flexibility.

PARENTAL RESPONSIBILITY

It is not easy to define according to academics. The starting point is statute but this does not give an adequate explanation of what these responsibilities actually are. Section 3(1) Children Act 1989 (CA 1989) states:

In this Act 'parental responsibility' means all the rights, duties, powers, responsibilities and authority which by law a parent of a child has in relation to the child and his property.

Case law provides a better source to assist in describing the precise nature of parental responsibility. Although parents' rights are not absolute and are decided on the basis of what is in the best interests of the child CA 1989 s 1(1). A court can override parental wishes.

Commentators have developed many examples of what is meant by parental responsibility. Lowe and Douglas have developed the following list:

- Bringing up a child
- Having contact with a child
- Protecting and maintaining the child
- Disciplining the child
- Determining and providing for the child's education
- Determining the child's religion
- Consenting to the child's medical treatment
- Consenting to the child's marriage
- Agreeing to the child's adoption
- Vetoing the issue of a child's passport
- Taking the child outside the UK and consenting to emigration
- Administering the child's property
- Protecting and maintaining the child
- Naming the child
- Representing the child in legal proceedings
- Disposing of the child's corpse
- Appointing a guardian for the child

All rights, duties, powers, responsibility and authority in relation to the child

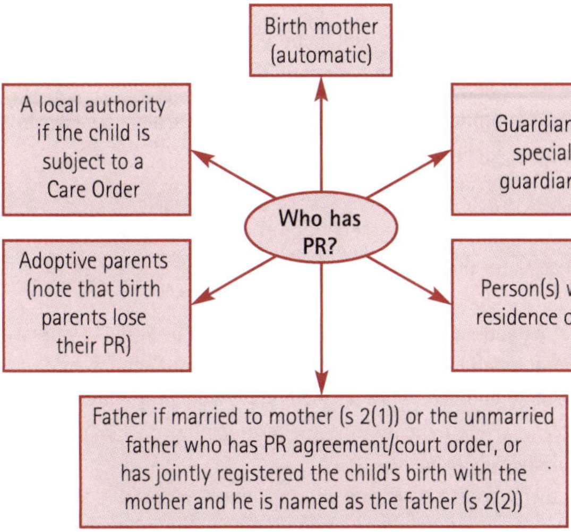

Person(s) with PR can act independently of others, except:

- if consent is required from all with PR;
- if this would be in contravention of a court order; or
- if PR is held as a result of a care order or by a special guardian
- if a child is sufficiently mature to make decisions for him or herself (the *Gillick* competent child)

Parental responsibility cannot be given away. The parents will retain it even if they divorce. If the child is made the subject of a care order, they will share it with the local authority, and they cannot transfer it to another party in an attempt to avoid their responsibilities.

Parental responsibility can be shared by more than one person. It continues after divorce, dissolution or if parents separate. It ends when a child reaches the age of majority, on adoption and in some circumstances by court order.

PR can be brought to an end by the child being adopted, resulting in the PR being vested in the adoptive parents. PR comes to an automatic end when the child reaches maturity, marries or joins the armed forces.

Often considered as more important than who is a parent, these topics are linked. More than one person can have parental responsibility.

Parental responsibility can be obtained 'automatically' in law in the following way by virtue of:

- All mothers automatically have parental responsibility
- Married parents – Children Act 1989 (CA 1989) section 2(1) (ie a father married to the mother)
- An unmarried mother – CA 1989 section 2(2)
- A mother and her civil partner who is a parent by virtue of the Human Fertilisation and Embryology Act 2008 – section 43 HFEA 2008
- The mother and her female partner who is a parent by virtue of section 43 HFEA 2008 – by registering the birth jointly, or by way of parental responsibility agreement.
- A mother who is a parent by virtue of the HFEA 2008 – section 43 (a mother who has a child by assisted reproduction)
- Parents whose marriage is void, provided that at the time of the marriage both of them reasonably believed the marriage to be valid
- Parents who marry after the child's birth are treated as if they were married at the time of the birth
- A father who is registered on the child's birth certificate as the father – CA 1989 section 4
- An unmarried father makes a 'parental responsibility agreement' with the mother – CA 1989 section 4(1)(b) (as amended)
- A father has been granted a residence order – s 12(1) CA 1989 under section 4
- A father has been appointed as guardian – CA 1989 section 5(6) or he has adopted a child

Person who can 'acquire' parental responsibility

- An unmarried father CA 1989 s 4 – by agreement or application to court
- A step-parent (whether by marriage or civil partnership) – CA 1989 s 4A

- A female non-biological parent in a same-sex female relationship – s 4ZA CA 1989

Unmarried fathers and parental responsibility

This has been and continues to be a controversial area of the law. You will find much commentary written about it and it can be a popular exam topic.

Unmarried fathers do not have automatic parental responsibility under CA 1989 s 2(2) and will need to acquire it through an agreement with the mother or via an application to the court. Any agreement must be made on a prescribed form available from HM Courts' Service and this form must be signed by both parents and witnessed & registered with the Principle Registry and Family Division (PRFD) London.

An application to court by an unmarried father is made under CA 1989 section 4(1)(c). When considering such an application the court will have regard to what is in the best interests of the child and due consideration will be given to the welfare principle CA 1989 section 1(1). The vast majority of applications made under section 4 CA 1989 are granted. Only in unusual cases will parental responsibility not be granted, although there is no presumption in favour of awarding *PR Re H (Parental Responsibility)* [1998].

The case of *Re H (Minors) (Local Authority: Parental Responsibility) No 3* [1991] listed the factors that are taken account of when considering an application for PR:

- Degree of commitment father has shown towards child
- The degree of attachment that exists between father and child
- The reason for the father applying for the order

Although each case depends on own facts and can include the following:

- Contact with the child – regular/financial support
- Status of father biologically?
- Child's reaction to failed application
- The child's view
- Misuse
- Parental responsibility and other orders
- Reprehensible contact of father

- Mother's reaction to granting of order
- Mother's death
- Father's ability to exercise parental responsibility
- Father's standing under the Hague convention – abduction fears

Unmarried fathers were not given automatic parental responsibility by the Children Act 1989 because Government considered it might be detrimental to some mothers.

Re H (Illegitimate Child: Father: Parental Rights) (No 2) [1991] 1 FLR 214

Position of the natural father can be infinitely variable, lower end of spectrum, one act of intercourse, possible rape, or top end of the spectrum, he may play a full role in the child's life, considerable evils might result if the father is at the bottom end of the spectrum had been given automatic parental responsibility.

Reform to the law has been proposed with regard to compulsory birth registration. New provisions contained in the Welfare Reform Act 2009/10 would make it compulsory for both unmarried parents to register the child's birth unless it is impractical, unreasonable or impossible. It is hoped this measure would result in more unmarried fathers gaining parental responsibility with the aim being to promote the involvement of both unmarried parents in a child's upbringing.

Non-parents

The rights/responsibilities obtained in these cases may differ:

- Those appointed to a child as guardian – CA 1989 s 5(6)
- When a person who is not a parent or guardian obtains a residence order, eg grandparent – *Re B (A Child)* [2009] UKSC 5, [2010]
- A person who is granted an emergency protection order (EPO)

GUARDIANS AND SPECIAL GUARDIANS

Under s 5 of the Children Act a guardian can be appointed by the court or by a parent to care for the child in the event of the parent's death. In the case of the latter appointment, it must be made in writing and must be dated and witnessed correctly. However, it must be noted that where the deceased parent has appointed a guardian, that appointment will only be effective if there is no other parent with PR, unless the deceased parent had a residence order in respect of the child. As indicated earlier, a guardian under s 5 will get PR for the child.

Special guardians are covered by ss 14A–F of the Children Act 1989. These orders are designed to be an alternative to adoption orders although it is unclear how successful they will be. The potential applicants, who must be over 18, are:

- a guardian under s 5 of the Children Act 1989;
- someone who has a residence order;
- someone with whom the child has lived for at least 3 years;
- a local authority foster parent who has had the child live with them for at least one year.

Before the court can make a special guardianship order they must be provided with a report by the local authority dealing with the applicant's suitability to be a special guardian.

If an order is made, the special guardian will obtain PR, but will also be able to limit the exercise of PR by any other PR holders, unless consent of all PR holders is needed by law (for example marriage). The order will last until the child is 18, unless ended earlier.

Additionally, if the order is granted, the local authority must provide services to the special guardian under the terms of section 14F of the Children Act. These services may therefore include financial support.

THE KEY PRINCIPLES UNDER THE CHILDREN ACT 1989

s 1(1) → The child's welfare is the court's *paramount* consideration when dealing with issues relating to the child's upbringing or the child's property. Does not apply to financial provisions for child support/ maintenance, Adoption Act 1976 application (note changes in Adoption and Children Act 2002), applications for leave (see later).

s 1(2) → Delay to be avoided in progressing cases, as deemed prejudicial to child's welfare. Planned, purposeful delay acceptable (*C v Solihull MBC* [1993]).

s 1(3) & 1(4) → Sets out the so called welfare checklist. A list of factors for the courts to assess what is in the welfare of the child, in the situations indicated by sub-s (4)

s 1(5) → The no-order principle. The court should not make an order under the CA 1989 unless they consider that making the order would be better for the child than making no order at all: *B v B (A Minor: Grandparents: Residence Order)* [1992].

The welfare checklist – s 1

Section 1(3) contains what has become commonly known as the 'checklist' – the factors that the court is required to consider when dealing with the circumstances mentioned in s 1(4).

These situations are:

- where the court is being asked to make, vary or discharge a s 8 order and this is disputed by one of the parties;
- where the court is considering whether to make, vary or discharge an order under Part IV (see later).

Whilst in other situations the court is not required to refer to the checklist, in reality this is frequently done.

WHAT SORT OF THINGS DOES THE COURT LOOK AT?

The ascertainable wishes and feelings of the child – s 1(3)(a)

This factor develops the philosophy of '*Gillick* competence' and is most important when a child is considered to be *Gillick* competent. The child's wishes will be judged in the light of his age and understanding. Sturge Glaiser (2000) have formulated the following in relation to age:

- The wishes of a child under the age of 6 are indistinguishable from that of the main carer.
- The wishes of a child over the age of 10 to carry considerable weight
- Children between the ages of 6–10 are at an intermediate age.

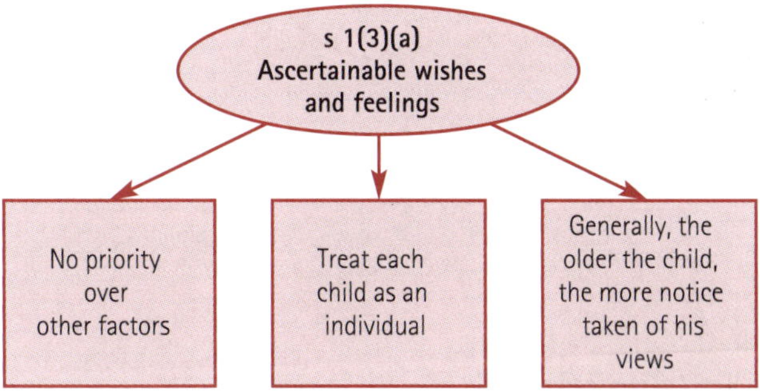

The child's physical, emotional and educational needs – s 1(3)(b)

The court will consider the closeness of the relationship with the parent(s) and child and the emotional needs of the child and how both parents are best able to meet these.

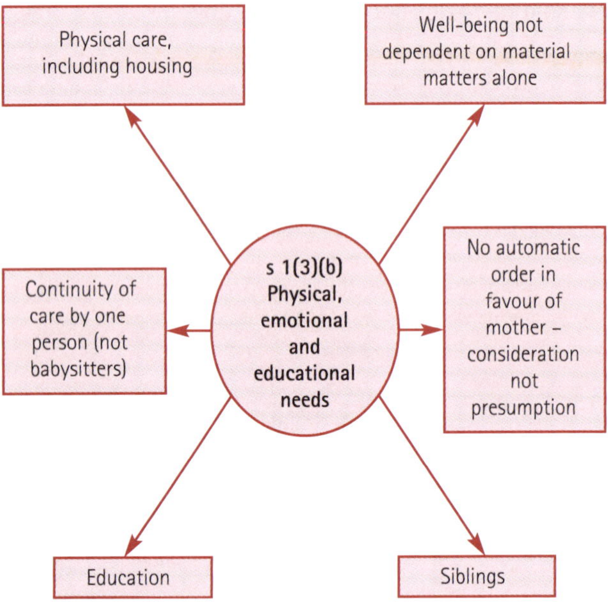

The likely effect on the child of any change in his circumstances – s 1(3)(c)

The Courts stress the importance of maintaining the status quo, the current arrangements for a child. This can lead to assertions that welfare principle is biased towards mothers, as the mother is usually the primary carer and where a child remains on the breakdown of a relationship. The status quo can also be disrupted in certain situations and case law supports this for example drug taking parents, a judge trying to ensure contact occurs or a third party preferred over natural parent. The court must also consider the impact of moving, changing schools and routines.

Good reasons will always be needed to change current arrangements or justify a move to another parent. These factors were considered in both *Re G* [2006], *Re B* [2009].

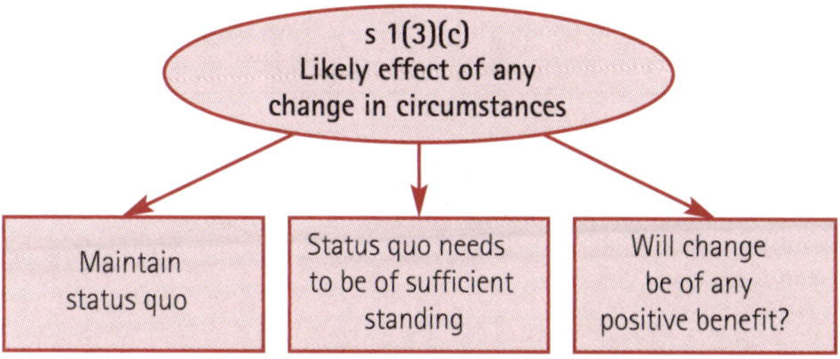

The child's sex, background and any characteristics which the court considers relevant – s 1(3)(d)

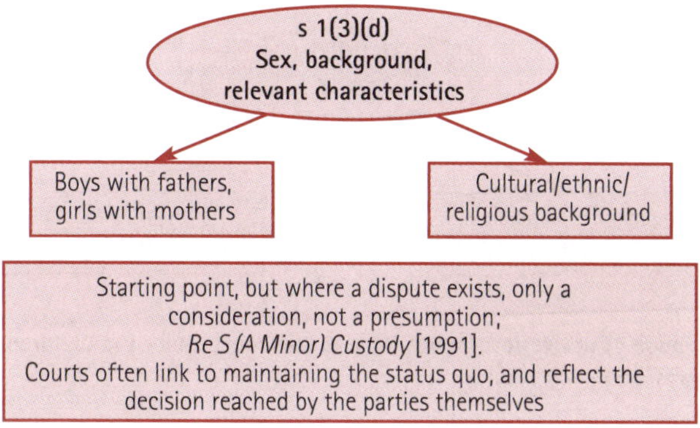

Any harm which the child has suffered or is at risk of suffering – s 1(3)(e)

Harm is defined in CA 1989 s 31(9) as ill-treatment or the impairment of health or development including impairment suffered by hearing or seeing ill-treatment. The courts must find proven facts on the balance of probability that reveal risk *Re M and R (Child Abuse: Evidence)* [1996]. Risk only needs to be a real possibility of harm and can include harm to a child's primary carer. It is not always easy to judge if a particular arrangement will cause harm to a child and this is always a challenge for the courts and professionals involved.

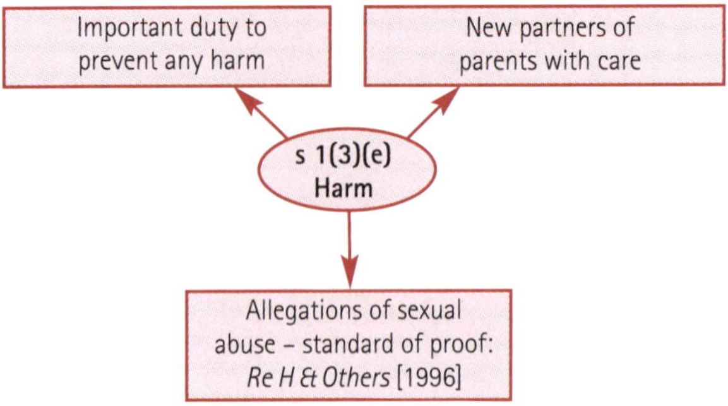

The capability of each parent to meet the child's needs – s 1(3)(f)

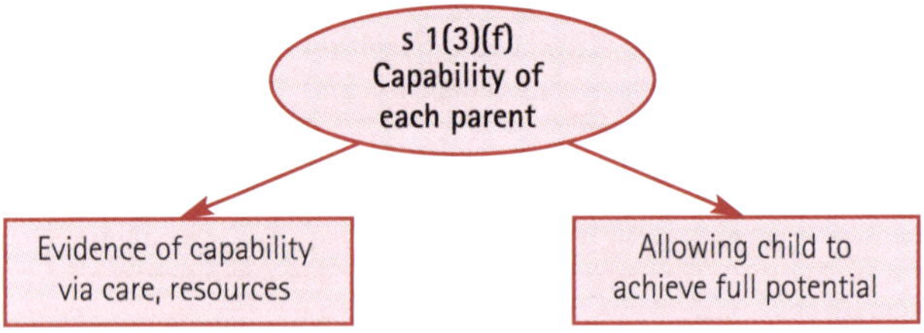

The range of powers/orders available to the court under the Children Act 1989

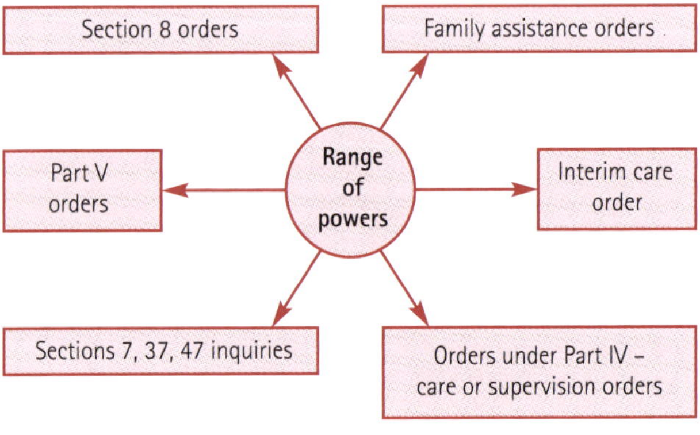

PRIVATE LAW ORDERS

These are the orders that the court is most likely to be asked to grant in proceedings between two individuals – that is, divorcing spouses or cohabiting couples that have separated. However, it is not unusual for a private law order to be made in proceedings commenced by the local authority, since the court must consider the full range of options available to it.

SECTION 8 ORDERS

The orders are:

- residence orders;
- contact orders;
- prohibited steps orders; and
- specific issues orders.

Section 10(1) of the Act gives the court the power to make s 8 orders in any family proceedings in which a question arises with respect to the welfare of any child if:

- an application for the order has been made by a person who:
  - is entitled to apply for a s 8 order with respect to the child; or
  - has obtained the leave of the court to make the application; or
- the court considers that the order should be made even though no such application has been made.

The first point of note is 'What are family proceedings?'. The definition is contained in section 8(3) and (4) CA 1989.

Section 8(3) Children Act 1989

For the purposes of this Act, 'family proceedings' means any proceedings:

(a) under the inherent jurisdiction of the High Court in relation to children; and

(b) under the enactments mentioned in sub-s (4), but does not include proceedings on an application for leave under s 100(3).

Section 8(4)

The enactments are:

(a) Parts I, II and IV of this Act;

(b) the MCA 1973;

(ba) Schedule 5 to the Civil Partnership Act 2004;

(d) the Adoption and Children Act 2002;

(e) the Domestic Proceedings and Magistrates' Courts Act 1978;

(ea) Schedule 6 to the Civil Partnership Act 2004;

(g) Part III of the Matrimonial and Family Proceedings Act 1984;

(h) the Family Law Act 1996;

(h) ss 11 and 12 of the Crime and Disorder Act 1998.

WHO CAN APPLY FOR S 8 ORDERS?

Section 10(4) Children Act 1989

The following persons are entitled to apply to the court for any s 8 order with respect to a child:

(a) any parent or guardian of the child;

(aa) any person who by virtue of section 4A has parental responsibility for the child;

(b) any person in whose favour a residence order is in force with respect to the child.

The definition of parenthood has been expanded both through the common law as can be seen in *Re G (Children)* [2006] UKHL 43 where the House of Lords held two lesbians to both be parents.

More recently under Part 2 of the Human Fertilisation and Embryology Act 2008 the law recognises mothers, fathers and 'other parents'. The Act takes account of parenthood status in assisted reproduction, the law relating to transferring parentage from the surrogate mother (will not be enacted until 2011) and the new parental order extending to commissioning civil partners of both genders and to some couples who are not married/not civil partners.

Section 10(5) Children Act 1989

The following persons are entitled to apply for a residence or contact order with respect to the child:

(a) any party to a marriage (whether or not subsisting), in relation to whom the child is a child of the family;

(aa) any civil partner in a civil partnership (whether or not subsisting) in relation to whom the child is a child of the family;

(b) any person with whom the child has lived for a period of at least three years;

(c) any person who:
   (i) in any case where a residence order is in force with respect to the child, has the consent of each of the persons in whose favour the order was made;
   (ii) in any case where the child is in the care of the local authority, has the consent of that authority;
   (iii) in any other case, has the consent of each of those (if any) who have parental responsibility for the child.

An example of the flexibility brought into the area of remedies available under the Children Act 1989 is the fact that any person can apply for a section 8 order. If they are not included in the above groups, then they must apply to the court for leave to apply for an order (s 10(1)(a)(ii)).

The factors that the court has to consider when dealing with an application for leave are contained in s 10(9) Children Act 1989:

(a) the nature of the proposed application for the s 8 order;

(b) the applicant's connection with the child;

(c) any risk of that proposed application disrupting the child's life to such an extent that he would be harmed by it; and

(d) where the child is being looked after by a local authority:
   (i) the authority's plans for the child's future; and
   (ii) the wishes and feelings of the child's parents.

Foster parents

A problem could arise under s 9(3) in cases where the child has been in foster care. Where the child is, or has been at any time within the last six months, in foster care, then the person who had care of the child (that is, the foster parent) may not apply for leave to apply for a s 8 order unless:

- he has the consent of the authority;
- he is a relative of the child; or
- the child has lived with him for at least three years preceding the application.

The time period mentioned in this restriction need not be continuous, but must have begun not more than five years before the making of the application.

When can children apply for s 8 orders?

A child needing advice may well be able to help himself by applying for a section 8 order.

He must apply for leave to apply for such an order, and the court, in order to grant leave, must be satisfied that the child has sufficient understanding to make the proposed application (*Gillick* test). This will obviously be judged on the age and maturity of the particular child involved in each case. Because of the difficulties which arise in these cases, such applications should be heard by the High Court (*Practice Direction (Application by Children: Leave)* [1993]).

Child applications for leave

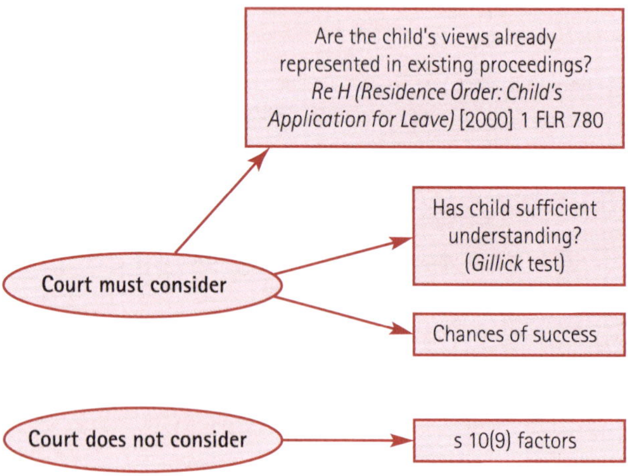

Restrictions on making s 8 orders

The court is limited in relation to section 8 orders in that they cannot be made in all situations:

s 9(6): court should not make a s 8 order to have effect after child has reached the age of 16 unless satisfied that the circumstances of the case are exceptional;

s 9(7): court should not make a s 8 order, other than varying or discharging such an order, with respect to a child who has reached the age of 16, unless satisfied that the circumstances of the case are exceptional.

Residence and contact orders are considered to be the primary orders in s 8 of the Act. Prohibited steps orders and specific issues orders are seen as secondary orders, as illustrated by the restrictions placed on their use by s 9(5).

By virtue of this sub-section, the court cannot exercise its power to make either order with a view to achieving a result which could be achieved by making a residence or contact order, or in any way which is denied to the High Court (by s 100(2)) in the exercise of its inherent jurisdiction with respect to children. It is said that it prevents the use of such orders in order to achieve certain aims via 'the back door' and ensures that the primary orders and inherent jurisdiction are used in the appropriate circumstances.

In *Nottinghamshire CC v P* [1993], it was held that a prohibited steps order which prevented contact between the father and the children and excluded the father from the family home could not be allowed to stand, as it was seen as achieving a result which could be achieved by the making of a residence or contact order, and the local authority was attempting to use the 'back door' approach to the problem.

RESIDENCE ORDERS

Residence orders (ROs) settle the arrangements to be made as to the person with whom the child is to live. This is detailed under section 8(1) Children Act 1989.

'An order settling the arrangements to be made as to the person with whom a child is to live.'

The necessity for an RO most frequently occurs in family breakdown situations and is used to settle disputes over what was previously known as custody. The intention behind the order is not just to decide who has possession of the child; it will also mean that they take on the everyday responsibilities of care for the child. Because of this, the matter of parental responsibility must be considered – in order to fulfil this task, the person with the RO must be able to take everyday decisions regarding the upbringing of the child. If an RO is granted to a married parent, then it will not alter the situation that each parent will retain parental responsibility and each is able to act independently for the benefit of the child. If the order is granted to an unmarried father, the court is obliged to grant him parental responsibility by way of a s 4 'parental responsibility order' (s 12(1)), which he will share with the mother.

A v A (Shared Residence) [2004] 1 FLR 1195

There had been bitter and lengthy proceedings between the parties. However, by the time this particular application got to court the children were spending approx 50 per cent of their time with each parent who lived close by to one another. The father had an interim sole residence order which he wanted confirmed and the mother wanted a joint order. The court held that although a sole residence order to the father would not, as a matter of law, diminish Mrs A's status it would be making a statement that although she shared residence that was not to be recognised in a court order. Therefore, the order must reflect the reality, both that the children shared their lives equally with each parent and that parents were equal in the eyes of the law.

If the order is granted to a non-parent, they will be granted shared parental responsibility with the parent (s 12(2)), but it will be limited, in as much as the non-parent will be unable to consent to or refuse to consent to an adoption or appoint a guardian (s 12(3)).

PRINCIPLES APPLIED BY THE COURT

Application of the welfare principle in residence applications

The key factor for any court is what is considered to be in the best interest of the child. In applying this principle the court frequently has to consider issues relating to the gestational, biological and psychological parent in the case.

Re G (Children) (Residence: Same Sex Parent) [2006] UKHL 43

> 'While CW is their psychological parent, CG is both their biological and their psychological parent. In the overall welfare judgment, this must count for something in the vast majority of cases. Its significance must be considered and assessed.' (Hale at para 38)

The case law shows differing judicial approaches to the weight accorded to genetic and non-genetic parents in residence cases. Good discussion on these points is evidenced in both *Re G (Children) (Residence: Same Sex Parent)* [2006] and *Re B (A Child) (Residence: Biological Parent)* [2009] UKSC 5.

Re B (A Child) (Residence: Biological Parent) [2009] UKSC 5

This case considered the respective role of parents and other persons in the life of a child for the purpose of making a residence order under CA 1989 section 8. This case involved a child where residence had been awarded to a grandparent. The decision was challenged by the father and then subsequently again by the grandmother. On appeal to the Supreme Court discussion focused on the role and manner in which persons fulfilled the role of parents. The judges were clear in this case that the consideration of the importance of parenthood assumed significance as only one of the contributing factors to the child's welfare. The Court of Appeal had been distracted by the natural/biological argument of the child's father and as a result due consideration had not been given to the child's welfare and what was considered to be in his best interests. Residence was then transferred to the grandmother. This case highlights the dangers of looking only to the genetic relationship of a child with regard to the natural biological parent to the detriment of considering what was actually in the best interests of the child.

Re B has given a clear statement of the law, any talk of presumptions or of the rights of the child to be cared for by the biological parents are wrong and will detract from an examination of what is in the best interests of the child. Everett and Yeatman, 'Are some parents more natural than others?' [2010] C.F.L.Q 22(3), 290–309.

The court considers other principles for example Very young children should live with their mothers.

However, this is a starting point for consideration, not a presumption: *Re S (A Minor) (Custody)* [1991].

Status Quo

The courts are keen to preserve the status quo unless there are good reasons for change in the child'circumstances: *Re B (Residence Order: Status Quo)* [1998] 1 FLR 368.

RE B (Residence Order: Status Quo) [1998] 1 FLR 368

The child had lived with his father since the break up of the parents. The court found that the mother would be the better parent for ensuring good contact; however, they declined to make a residence order in her favour as they considered that preserving the status quo was seen as vital to the child's well-being. Accordingly the child was left with his father.

Shared Residence Orders

These orders are made in favour of two people who live in separate places and specify the amount of time a child is required to spend with each individual (parent) eg alternate weeks with mother and father. Commentary to be found on this issue in *Re G (Children) (Residence: Same Sex Parent)* [2006] UKHL.

These orders are considered under:

CA 1989 s 11(4) Where a residence order is made in favour of two or more persons who do not themselves all live together, the order may specify the periods during which the child is to live in the different households concerned.

To enable the courts to consider a shared residence order each parent should see the child between 30–70% of the time. The courts determine the correct division of time between each parent and then decide if a shared RO is appropriate in the circumstances.

Re K (Shared Residence Order) [2008]

In this case a child with Down's Syndrome was born to unmarried parents, the father was awarded contact time of 40%. The Court of Appeal granted a shared residence order because, as Wall LJ reiterates; 'Such an order emphasises the fact that both parents are equal in the eyes of the law and that they have equal duties and responsibilities as parents. The order can have the additional advantage of conveying the court's message that neither parent is in control and that the court expects parents to co-operate with each other for the benefit of their children.'

Although in some instances separate residence and contact orders are preferable on the facts of the time spent with each parent and the facts of the case and in the light of what is considered to be in the best interests of the child section 1(1) CA 1989. It should be noted that a residence order will cease if the parents live together for more than six months.

Limits on residence orders

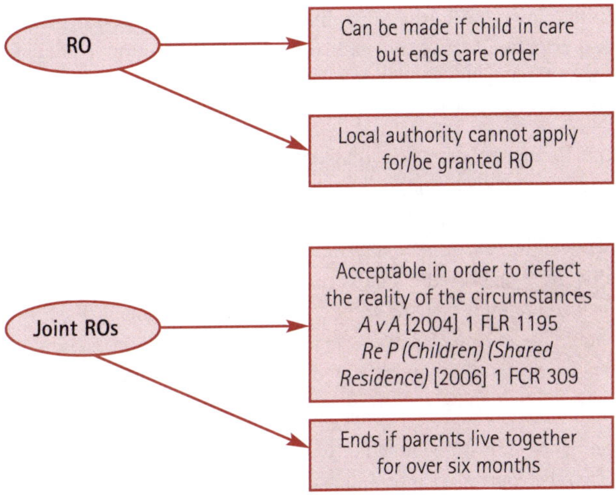

Following the granting of a residence order, s 13 of the Act must be considered. It states that, if such an order is in force, no person may:

- cause the child to be known by a new surname; or
- remove him from the UK for over one month,

without the written consent of every person who has parental responsibility for the child or the leave of the court.

With regard to changing the child's surname, the court must be involved not only if there is an RO in existence, but also where any parent, with or without PR, objects to the change. The child's best interests will be of prime importance together with the reasons for seeking the change (*Dawson v Wearmouth* [1999]). If the child is old enough, their views will be taken into account. The courts are increasingly taking a very pragmatic approach in these cases (*Re (A Child)* [2001]).

DAWSON v WEARMOUTH [1999] 1 FLR 1167

Mr and Mrs W had married and divorced after having two children together. Mrs W then met a new partner and had a third child. Shortly after the third child was born Mrs W left the father and registered the child with the name Wearmouth. The father applied for a prohibited steps order to prevent the registration and a specific issue order regarding the child's name.

The House of Lords held that initial registration was a matter of great importance and therefore changing it was important and should be determined by the court where there is any dispute between the parties. No disputed change should be made unilaterally. In deciding the matter the courts should not distinguish between parents with or without parental responsibility. Each case should be decided on its own facts weighing up the factors and bearing in mind any benefit to the welfare of the child.

Again, when considering whether to grant leave for the child to leave the country, the court must bear in mind s 1, that is, the welfare and 'no order' principles. The cases which occur in this area often concern a family wishing to emigrate with the child.

CONTACT ORDERS SECTION 8 CA 1989

This is an order requiring the person with whom the child lives, or is to live, to allow the child to visit or to stay with the person named in the order, or for the named person and the child otherwise to have contact with each other. Section 8(1) CA 1989:

Means an order requiring the person with whom a child lives, or is to live, to allow the child to visit or stay with the person named in the order, or for that person and the child otherwise to have contact with each other.

M v M [1973] →

Traditional view
Contact with parents is the right of the child, not of the parents.

Post-Human Rights Act 1998
Contact is a right of both the child and the parents and the court's role is to establish whose right is greater (*Hendricks v Netherlands* [1983]; *B v UK* [1988]).

The order covers the area formerly known as access. It allows the non-resident parent or any other person named in the order to retain contact with the child, in a way to be decided by the court. Contact can be direct or indirect by way of stays, visits, letters, emails or telephone calls, depending on the circumstances of the case. Indirect contact may be channelled through an intermediary if necessary: *Re F (Indirect Contact)* [2007] 1 FLR 1015.

Court's attitude to contact

When reaching its decision on the matter of contact, the court must bear in mind that the paramount consideration is the welfare of the child. If there is conflict between the parties, the s 1(3) checklist must also be borne in mind. The key issue for the court is whether or not contact is considered to be in the best interests of the child CA 1989 section 1(1) and will contact promote the welfare of the child. A balancing exercise of the provisions laid down in CA 1989 section 1(3) is undertaken by the court. This is frequently the case, as these orders are usually sought in cases of family breakdown – bitterness and resentment can lead to a failure to reach an amicable agreement.

The accepted approach to the subject of contact is that there is a presumption that the child will be benefited by retaining contact with both parents. *Re O (Contact: Withdrawal of Application)* [2004] 1 FLR 1258 per Wall J, 'Unless there are cogent reasons against it, the children of separated parents are entitled to know and have the love and society of both their parents.'

Current law on contact considers the advantages and disadvantages of contact in each particular case and it is accepted that there is no presumption in favour of contact, although the benefits of contact can be evidenced in appropriate cases, the benefit can also be displaced in others. (Herring)

Re T (A Minor)(Parental Responsibility: Contact) [1993] Butler-Sloss at para 459:

> 'It is the general proposition, underpinned undoubtedly by the Children Act 1989 – and indeed the father has correctly reminded us of the importance of continuing relationships between children and their parents – that it is in the best interests of a child to retain contact with the parent whom the child does not reside. The courts generally set their face against depriving a child of such contact and urge reluctant care-taking parents to make contact work, however difficult it may be for that parent who very often does not understand the importance of that continuing contact.'

Re M (Contact: Welfare Test) [1995] para 275:

> 'Whether the fundamental emotional need of every child to have an enduring relationship with both his parents CA 1989 s1(3)(b) is outweighed by the depth of harm which in the light, inter alia of his wishes and feelings, CA 1989 s1(3)(a) this child would be at risk of suffering CA 1989 s1(3(e) by virtue of a contact order.'

Re Bradford [2006]; *Re O'Connell* [2007] per Wall LJ at para 70:

(1) that contact with a non-resident parent is in the best interests of children and (2) that it requires compelling evidence for such contact to be refused.

Contact should be allowed unless it can be shown to be detrimental to the child's welfare, as was illustrated in *Re H (Minors) (Access)* [1992].

RE H (A MINOR) (Parental Responsibility) [1993] 1 FLR 484

The step-father of the child had written to the father saying that contact with the now 2-year-old would put the marriage at risk. The parents had separated when the child was only 3 months old and although the father had regular contact until he was

7 months old the mother then stopped all contact because of her impending marriage. The father later applied for, and got contact for, a few months. This upset the step-father who then wrote to the father saying that he could 'have the mother back' as contact upset him so much!

The court held that the father should be denied contact because the risk posed to the new family unit clearly conflicted with the child's best interests.

Of particular concern is the question of direct contact in cases of domestic violence, primarily where the child is not a victim but may have observed violence or the caring parent is at risk. It had been suggested that the courts were ignoring or reducing the impact of violence, or fears of it, and ordering contact due to the presumption of automatic benefit. Following the publication of *Making Contact Work* (Consultation Paper (2001)) and the *Final Report* (2002), together with the decision in *Re L, Re V, Re M, Re H* [2000], the courts are more reluctant to order contact where domestic violence is an issue without first considering the evidence very carefully.

RE L; RE V; RE M; RE H (Contact: Domestic Violence) [2000] 2 FLR 334

The Official Solicitor asked two consultant psychiatrists to prepare a report for consideration on contact issues generally. In all four cases the father of children had been refused direct contact against a background of domestic violence. On appeal all four lost their case. The Court of Appeal held that there is no presumption or assumption against contact in domestic violence cases and generally it is in a child's best interests to have contact with the non-resident parent. However, the cases should distinguish where contact is sought in order to maintain an existing relationship, to revive a relationship, or to create one from scratch. The assumption of contact should decrease as you go across the spectrum. The ability of the father to recognise his past conduct, be aware of the need to change and to make genuine efforts to do so are all important considerations.

It is clear that in exceptional circumstances a contact order under s 8 can include an order for 'no-contact' (*Nottinghamshire CC v P (No 2)* [1993]). Applications for contact will be denied altogether where to allow contact would risk the child's welfare by destabilising the child's family unit; *Re H (A Minor) (Parental Responsibility)* [1993] 1 FLR 484.

Contact can be bitterly contested and in a minority of cases becomes impossible to resolve satisfactorily. These cases are known to the courts as 'intractable' and have often been seen to evidence a resident parent's opposition to contact, the resident parent most frequently being the mother.

Re S (A Child) (Transfer of Residence: Consent Order) [2010] EWHC 192 (Fam)

A disputed contact case spanning the whole life of S's life. Professional couple separated before the birth of S. Contact applied for by non-resident father and established and maintained until 2006 when it broke down. Mother continually refused to support contact. Applications by the father to the court culminated in the court ordering a transfer of residence to father in January 2010. Child removed from mother temporarily to foster parents to facilitate contact. Child refused to have any form of interaction with father despite extensive support from professionals. Despite best will of the courts to support and facilitate contact it was not successful and father agreed to S returning to live with mother and not making any more applications for contact.

Section 11(7) allows the court to attach directions as to how s 8 orders are to be carried out and to attach conditions: *Re O (Contact: Imposition of Conditions)* [1995]. In this case, indirect contact was ordered and a condition was imposed that the mother should allow letters to be sent to the child and allow presents sent by the father to be opened. She was also to send photographs of the child and information relating to school reports, etc, to the father.

Enforcement of contact

The enforcement of contact orders are problematic in a variety of ways, from the caring parent not handing the child over, to the person entitled to contact not taking it up. With regard to the former, the courts have a variety of options, from altering the order to try to get something that is workable, through to changing the RO, or ultimately committing the non-co-operative parent to prison – *A v N (Committal: Refusal of Contact)* [1997]. With the latter, it is much harder to establish a mechanism whereby the non-resident parent can be forced to attend for contact, and statistics show a dramatic reduction in the numbers of fathers who maintain contact after a period of two years. As contact is a right of the child, and given the State's responsibility to protect individuals' rights under the European Convention on Human Rights, some method of enforcement should be considered. This has been noted in the *Making Contact Work* documents referred to above.

The courts have been far more ready to admit that the existing system for enforcing contact does not serve parents well (see *Re D (Intractable Contact Dispute Publicity)* [2004]). Hence the courts have been increasingly inventive in seeking ways to ensure contact takes place.

Additionally, the Children Act has been amended by the Children and Adoption Act 2006 with the insertion of sections 11A–11P. Essentially, parents can now be ordered to attend programmes, classes and counselling in order to assist them in seeing that their behaviour is harmful and they must therefore co-operate for their child's welfare.

Supervised contact

All the parties named in a s 16 family assistance order (FAO), with the exception of the child, must consent to the order being made. The maximum duration of an FAO is six months, which can limit the utility of the order in these circumstances.

PROHIBITED STEPS ORDERS

These are defined in the Act as:

> . . . an order that no step which could be taken by a parent in meeting his parental responsibility for a child and which is of the kind specified in the order.

It will be seen that the order covers steps which fall within the area of parental responsibility. As such, it is to some extent limited in its application, in as much as it cannot be used to prevent steps which would not come within this ambit, for example, assault or molestation; other measures would be needed in those circumstances.

This type of order is intended to deal with individual or single issues in a particular case, and is meant to prevent a particular step being taken. A common example would be an order preventing the removal of a child from the UK in a case where there was no residence order in force, and so no prohibition under s 13 to prevent such removal.

Relocation

Within the jurisdiction

Where one parent has the residence order there is no legal duty upon them to consult the other parent when making a decision to relocate the family home. The courts are reluctant to interfere with a parent's decision to relocate except in exceptional circumstances. *Re E (Minors) (Residence: Conditions)* [1997] 2 FLR 638. The court may intervene where the child's welfare would be put at risk if the move was allowed: *Re S (A Child) (Residence Order Conditions) (No 2)* [2003] 1 FLR 138.

In *Re F (Internal Relocation)* [2010]

A mother applied to move her 4 children from the North east of England to one of the Orkney Islands. Her application to remove the children ranging in age from 9 to 14 years of age, was refused.

'In the light of the gross upheaval which the move would precipitate for the children and of the fact that, in the case of G and T and to a lesser extent of A, the mother would be imposing upon the children, even at their relatively advanced ages, permanent living arrangements entirely contrary to their own wishes, the recorder was in my view entitled to forecast emotional strain and indeed harm for them.' At para 36.

This case highlighted the fact that it was considered perhaps unfortunate that an exceptionality test had developed with regard to internal relocation.

Outside the jurisdiction

It has long been the court's approach not to interfere with reasonable decisions of the parent with the RO to leave the jurisdiction (*Poel v Poel* [1970] 1 WLR 1469). However, there is no presumption in favour of the applicant parent. There should be a genuine motivation for the move and not the intention to end contact with the non-resident parent (*Payne v Payne* [2001]). In some cases it may be beneficial to the non-resident parent for the move to go ahead (*Re B (Leave to Remove)* [2007] 1 FLR 333). In *Re F (Internal Relocation)*.

Welfare principle in leave to remove applications

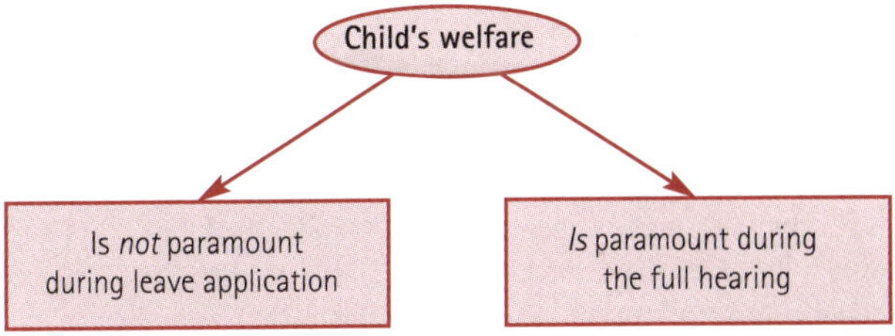

PAYNE v PAYNE [2001] 1 FLR 1052

The Court of Appeal provided guidelines for the courts to consider in leave to remove cases:

(a) The welfare of the child is always paramount.
(b) There is no presumption created by s 13(1)(b) in favour of the applicant parent.
(c) The reasonable proposals of the parent with a residence order wishing to live abroad carry great weight.
(d) Consequently the proposals have to be scrutinised with care and the court needs to be satisfied that there is a genuine motivation for the move and not the intention to bring contact between the child and the other parent to an end.
(e) The effect upon the applicant parent and the new family of the child of a refusal of leave is very important.
(f) The effect upon the child of the denial of contact with the other parent and in some cases his family is very important.
(g) The opportunity for continuing contact between the child and the parent left behind may be very significant.

In a more recent case *Re AR (A Child: Relocation)* [2010] a mother (M) applied to remove her 5 year old son to France. The father (F) opposed the application. This case provides a useful discussion of the factors for consideration set out in

Payne v Payne [2001], including their relevance some ten years on and application to the facts of this case. The court summarised the considerations as follows at para 54:

(a) Is M's application genuine in the sense that it is not motivated by some selfish desire to exclude F from A's life? Is M's application realistic, founded on practical proposals both well researched and investigated?

(b) Is F's opposition motivated by genuine concern for the future of A's welfare or is it driven by some ulterior motive? What would be the extent of the detriment to him and his future relationship with A were the application granted? To what extent would that be offset by extension of A's relationships with the maternal family and homeland?

(c) What would be the impact on M of a refusal of her realistic proposal?

(d) The paramountcy principle as directed by the statutory checklist.

In this case the mother's application to remove her son from the UK was refused. The judge made a shared residence order at para 52.

'I am clearly of the view that a joint or shared residence order should be made. Indeed, such an order is nowadays the rule rather than the exception even where the quantum of care undertaken by each parent is decidedly unequal. There is very good reason why such orders should be normative for they avoid the psychological baggage of right, power and control that attends a sole residence order, which was the one of the reasons that we were ridden of the notions of custody and care and control by the Act of 1989. A joint/shared residence order is not inapt even if leave to relocate is granted: see Re G.'

SPECIFIC ISSUES ORDER

This is defined as:

> . . . an order giving a direction for the purpose of determining a specific question which has arisen or which may arise in connection with any aspect of parental responsibility for a child.

Again, it will be seen that it is normally intended to deal with a single issue, and so is similar to a prohibited steps order. It is also limited by the requirement that the matter be within the area of parental responsibility. Where there is a dispute between the parents on a specific matter, the court can resolve the matter by considering the welfare principle and checklist and granting an order stating the necessary course of action. Common areas of conflict are:

1 The issue of a child's education, as was the case in *Re P (A Minor) (Education: Child's Views)* [1992].
2 Medical treatment as in *Re J* [2000] 1 FLR 511 and *Re HG (Specific Issue: Sterilisation)* [1993].
3 The child's religion (Specific Issue Orders: Child's Religious Upbringing and Circumcision) [2000].
4 Paternity.

RE J (Specific Issue Orders: Child's Religious Upbringing and Circumcision) [2000] 1 FLR 571

A non-resident Muslim father wished his child to be circumcised, but the mother objected. Because the operation was not medically necessary, was irreversible and carried with it a small degree of risk, the Court of Appeal upheld the view that 'it must, therefore, join the exceptional categories where disagreement between holders of parental responsibility must be submitted to the court for determination.'

FAMILY ASSISTANCE ORDER

A new type of order introduced by the Children Act 1989 is the FAO, contained in s 16 of the Act.

In family proceedings, the court can make an FAO requiring either a probation officer or a local authority officer, usually a social worker, to be made available to advise, assist and befriend any person named in the order. However, before the order can be made, the local authority must agree to making the officer available (s 16(7)).

The persons who can be named in the order are those mentioned in s 16(2). They are:

- the child himself;
- the parent or guardian of the child;
- any person with whom the child is living or who has a contact order in his favour in respect of the child.

With the exception of the child, these persons, when named in the order, are also required to consent to the order being made (s 16(3)). The order can only be made for a limited duration and will only be available in exceptional circumstances.

This order will only be made by the court on its own motion and no applications can be made for this type of order. Due to the limited time scale and the difficulties in getting a social worker appointed, whilst the making of the order may be seen as best practice, in reality these orders are little used.

You should now be confident that you would be able to tick all of the boxes on the checklist at the beginning of this chapter. To check your knowledge of Children I why not visit the companion website and take the Multiple Choice Question test. Check your understanding of the terms and vocabulary used in this chapter with the flashcard glossary.

6

Children II

SOCIAL SERVICE INVESTIGATIONS

A local authority social services department (LA) has a range of obligations under the Children Act (CA) 1989, to assist and provide services to *children in need*, and to ensure that children are protected from abusive situations wherever possible (s 17). In order to enable the LA to decide what steps, if any, to take in relation to a child, the CA 1989 gives them a power of investigation under s 47. The duty to investigate a child's situation arises if:

- the child is subject to an emergency protection order (EPO) granted in favour of an applicant other than the LA;
- the child is subject to police protection under s 46;*
- the LA has reasonable cause to suspect that the child is suffering or is likely to suffer significant harm.

The purpose of the investigation will be to:

- see if the LA should apply for an order under the CA 1989 to safeguard and protect the child;
- see if a child subject to an EPO, who is not being provided with local authority accommodation, should be so provided;
- see if a child subject to police protection should be made subject to an EPO.

To carry out an effective investigation the LA should see the family and seek evidence of significant harm, and establish what action is needed to prevent the child suffering significant harm.

*Section 46 of the Children Act 1989 empowers a police officer who has reasonable cause to believe that a child would otherwise be likely to suffer significant harm, to:

- remove the child to suitable accommodation and keep him/her there; or
- take such steps as are reasonable to ensure that the child's removal from any hospital, or other place, in which he/she is being accommodated is prevented.

The child is considered to be in police protection when these powers have been exercised by the police.

Notes

1 Police powers under section 46 cannot be exercised unless and until a child is found.

2 A constable does not have the right to enter and search premises to remove a child without a warrant. (Section 17(1)(e) of the Police and Criminal Evidence Act 1984 gives adequate powers that may be executed where there is a need to save life or limb.)

3 The Children Act legislation implies the power to use reasonable force in appropriate circumstances to take a child into police protection or to keep the child there. The use of reasonable force is further supported by the decision of the divisional court in the case of *R v Commissioner of Police for the Metropolis* [2006].

SHORT-TERM ORDERS

CHILD ASSESSMENT ORDERS

Requirements

Grounds (s 43(1)):

- the applicant has reasonable cause to suspect that the child is suffering/ likely to suffer significant harm;

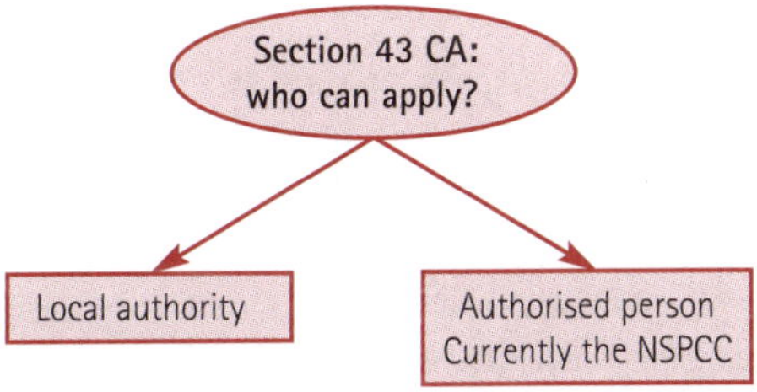

- an assessment of the state of the child's health or development or of the way in which he has been treated is required to enable the applicant to determine whether or not the child is suffering or is likely to suffer significant harm; and

- it is unlikely that such an assessment will be made or be satisfactory in the absence of an order under this section.

The court, being the Family Proceedings Court, will base its decision on the child's welfare and the order will require the parents or carers to produce the child for assessment or allow the child to be visited in order for an assessment to be carried out. This means that the child can remain with the family whilst any assessment is carried out. If the child has to go elsewhere for assessment, for example, a hospital, and has to stay away from home for a few days, then the court can give directions as to contact and may specify the length of time he can be kept there.

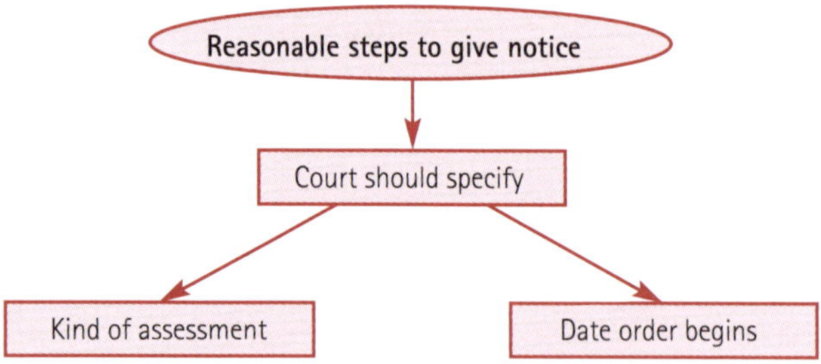

Duration: seven days maximum

The order should also specify how to make the assessment, but a child of sufficient understanding can refuse to undergo any form of assessment contained in the order (s 43(8)).

If the parents refuse to comply with the assessment order, there appears to be no direct form of enforcement. However, the local authority could inform them that, if they continue to fail to comply with the order, it could lead to the authority making an application for an EPO.

An important point to bear in mind when considering an assessment order is that, if the court thinks that grounds exist for the granting of an EPO, it may treat the application as an application for an emergency protection order and grant the order if the grounds are shown to exist (s 43(4)). There are problems with this sort of order, as it focuses on assessment and does not really have a protective element – it is more of an evidence gathering order. The order is used very infrequently and would seem to be utilised more as a threat to gain parents' co-operation in an investigation.

EMERGENCY PROTECTION ORDERS (EPOS)

These are short-term protective orders which permit the applicant (normally the LA) to remove the child to a safe environment. There are three different grounds upon which an order can be made. As with the CAO, applications will be made to the Family Proceedings Court.

s 44(1)(a)

Applicant – Any person (includes LA).

Criteria – There is reasonable cause to believe that the child is likely to suffer significant harm if he is not removed to accommodation provided by the applicant or he does not remain where he is currently accommodated.

A restrictive approach has been taken in the caselaw: *X Council v B (Emergency Protection Orders)* [2005] 1 FLR 341 – imminent danger must be established.

X COUNCIL v B (Emergency Protection Orders) [2005] 1 FLR 341

Emergency Protection orders were sought in relation to three children who were suffering physical, emotional and behavioural problems due to the significant levels of stress and distress in the family.

The High Court held that EPOs are draconian requiring exceptional justification and extraordinarily compelling reasons. Such an order should not be made unless the court is satisfied that it is both necessary and proportionate and that no other less radical form of order will achieve the essential end of promoting the welfare of the child. Separation is only to be contemplated if immediate separation is essential to secure the child's safety; imminent danger must be actually established. Moreover, the evidential burden on the local authority is even heavier if the application is made ex parte. Those who seek relief ex parte are under a duty to make the fullest and most candid and frank disclosure of all the relevant circumstances known to them.

s 44(1)(b)

Applicant – LA.

Criteria – LA is carrying out a s 47 Investigation and its enquiries are being frustrated by access to the child being denied and the applicant has reasonable cause to believe access is needed as a matter of urgency.

s 44(1)(c)
Applicant – NSPCC.

Criteria – The applicant has reasonable cause to suspect that the child is suffering or is likely to suffer significant harm.

The applicant is making enquiries.

The enquiries are being frustrated by access being denied.

Access is needed as a matter of urgency.

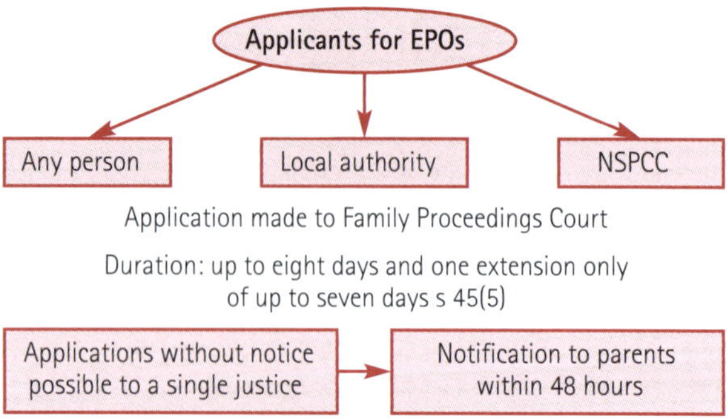

The effects of an Emergency Protection Order

Section 44(4) allows the court to direct any person who is in a position to do so to produce the child to the applicant and authorises their removal to, or retention in, accommodation provided by the applicant, or prevent the removal of the child from some other place where he was being accommodated immediately prior to the order.

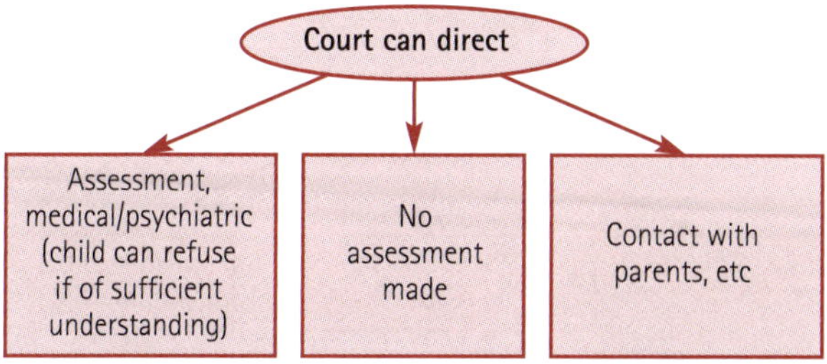

EPO gives applicant PR for duration of the order but limits its use to safeguarding the child's welfare

It is an offence to prevent the removal of the child or to obstruct a person exercising the power to remove the child. The authority should only remove the child from his home for as long as is necessary for the child's welfare and should return him home as soon as it is safe to do so. However, if the applicant considers that he needs to remove the child again during the existence of the order, he has the power to do so (s 44(10) and (12)).

The FLA 1996 has added s 44A to the CA 1989, which allows an exclusion requirement to be added to an EPO so that action is taken against the person alleged to be endangering the child, if the court has reasonable cause to believe that, if a person is excluded from a dwelling house in which the child lives:

- where the order is based on s 44(1)(a), (b) or (c);
- a person living in the dwelling house is to be able and willing to give to the child the care which it would be reasonable to expect a parent to give him and is to consent to the requirement.

The effect of the order is to require the person to leave the home, prohibit re-entry and exclusion from a defined area.

Applying to discharge the order

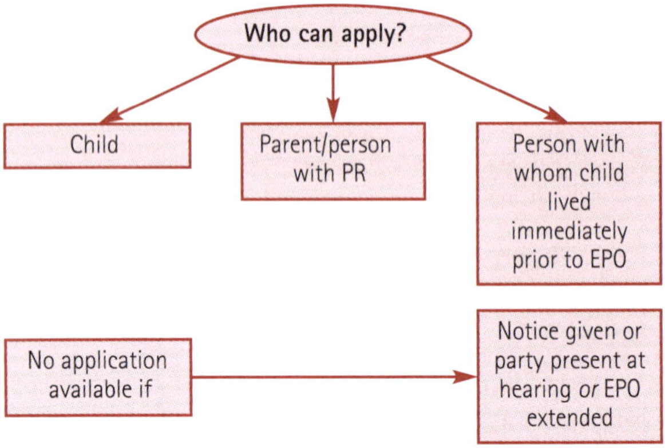

There is no appeal against an EPO, but parents may apply to discharge it after 72 hours have elapsed (if the order is without notice) (s 45(9)).

CARE AND SUPERVISION ORDERS

Since the Children Act 1989 came into effect, there is now only one way in which a child can be placed into the care of a local authority or be made the subject of a supervision order. This is by the applicant being able to satisfy the requirements of s 31(2) of the Act and showing that the welfare of the child demands that the order be made. Wardship can no longer be used to make a child the subject of these orders. Once an application has been made to the court under s 31(1), the court has the power to make either a care order (CO) or a supervision order (SO) if the LA has proven the 'threshold criteria'. (Alternatively, the court can consider granting a s 8 residence order – but not in favour of the LA.)

Re: B [2008] UKHL 35 is concerned with s 31(2) and the difficulty of proving when a child 'is likely to suffer significant harm' and how the court is likely to be satisfied with whether or not this will happen. There are two possibilities here: firstly, a 'real possibility' test in which case the court would overrule the previous decision of the House of Lords in *Re H (Minors) (Sexual Abuse: Standard of Proof)* [1996] AC 563; or alternatively, should facts be proved in the normal way on the balance of probabilities?

The House of Lords rejected the appeal, holding that disputed facts were either proven on the balance of probabilities or unproven in which case those facts are established as having not occurred. They also pointed out that the burden of proof in civil cases cannot be artificially heightened in the most serious cases of abuse.

Re H (Minors) (Sexual Abuse: Standard of Proof) [1996] AC 563

Four sisters. Eldest alleged that she had been sexually abused by step-father over a number of years. He was prosecuted in the criminal court but was acquitted. LA then brought care proceedings in relation to the three younger girls, relying on the lower standard of proof in civil proceedings and arguing there was a risk of harm to the three girls arising out of the alleged sexual abuse of their sister. The judge was not satisfied that the abuse had occurred, referring to the 'high standard of proof' required for a care order.

The question before the HL was: 'When a local authority assert but fail to prove past misconduct, can the judge's suspicions or lingering doubts on that issue form the basis for concluding that the second limb of s31(2)(a) has been made out?' (i.e. likely to suffer significant harm).

The majority held that it could not. The HL decided:

- 'likely' in s 31(2)(a) just means 'a real possibility' of future harm ie 'a possibility that cannot sensibly be ignored having regard to the nature and gravity of the feared harm in the particular case' (*per* Lord Nicholls). It does *not* require the court to be satisfied that harm is 'more likely than not' to happen.
- The relevant time to assess this is when the LA first intervenes (as per *Re H* above).
- The ordinary civil standard of proof applies: the court must be satisfied on a balance of probabilities (more likely than not) that harm is 'likely'. In other words, it must be satisfied that it is more likely than not that harm is a real possibility.

  (Thus a child can be removed even if he himself hasn't yet been harmed so long as the court decides, on a balance of probabilities, that future harm is a real possibility.)

  Note the burden of proof is on the LA.
- Majority: If the case is based on a likelihood of future harm the court must be satisfied on a balance of probabilities that the facts upon which

that prediction was based did actually happen. Suspicion will not be enough.

- Minority: A number of suspicious facts, albeit unproven, could when taken together be probative of likelihood of such harm.

All care proceedings will commence in the Family Proceedings Court, but matters may be transferred to a designated county court or the High Court if it is considered appropriate, since all these courts have jurisdiction to deal with care matters as they fall within the definition of 'family proceedings'.

Who can apply for a care or supervision order?

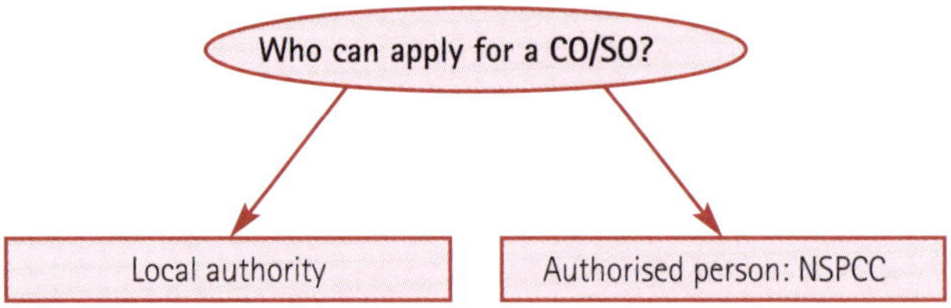

If the court is dealing with matters which are considered to be 'family proceedings' and it considers that a local authority should investigate the circumstances of the case, it has the power to direct that the authority should do so (s 37(1)).

However, if the authority carries out the investigation but decides that an application for a care order is not, in its opinion, necessary, then the court cannot require the authority to make an application. This could mean that situations may arise where children are left without measures available to safeguard their welfare, as occurred in the case of *Nottinghamshire CC v P* [1993].

A CO or SO can only be made in respect of a child who is under 17 years of age (or 16 if the child is married).

THE THRESHOLD CRITERIA

When the local authority has decided that an application is to be made, then it must be able to fulfil the requirements of s 31(2), which have become known as the '*threshold criteria*'.

Both parts needs to be satisfied

The child is suffering or is likely to suffer significant harm

+

Causation: the harm is attributable to –
(a) the level of care not being what it would be reasonable to expect a parent to give
or
(b) the child being beyond parental control

This is a strict test and unless the criteria are satisfied the court cannot intervene.

A vital element to remember is that, even when the authority has been able to satisfy the 'threshold criteria', the court will be required to consider the contents of s 1 of the Act.

The welfare, delay and 'no order' principles must be borne in mind before the final decision is made. They form the basis of the court's decision in all 'family proceedings'.

Section 31(9) contains the definitions of the terms used in the threshold criteria:

Harm – Ill treatment or the impairment of health and development

Development – Physical, intellectual, emotional, social or behavioural development

Health – Physical or mental health

Ill treatment – Includes sexual abuse and other forms of ill treatment which are not physical

Other definitions

Significant – Considerable, noteworthy or important: *Humberside CC v B* [1993]

Care – Normal physical and emotional care that a reasonable parent would give

The threshold for intervention

Test to apply to s 31(10)

When looking at the effect of any failings relating to the health and development of the child, s 31(10) states that the child in question must be judged against what can be expected of a similar child, having taken into account the characteristics of that child; that is, the court must take a subjective view of the child in question and apply an objective test when comparing him with a similar child.

The point in time against which the threshold criteria are assessed

In practice by the time the full proceedings are heard in court the child will have been in temporary accommodation with foster parents for some weeks, if not months, and therefore may no longer be said to be suffering or likely to suffer significant harm.

Therefore the House of Lords' decision in *Re M (A Minor) (Care Order: Threshold Conditions)* [1994] stated that the time when judgment about significant harm being suffered has to be made is when the local authority commences proceedings for the protection of the child, in other words, the time that the LA takes to initiate protection proceedings.

RE M (A Minor) (Care Order: Threshold Conditions) [1994] 3 ALL ER 298

M, who had three older siblings, was 4 months old when his father murdered his mother in front of all the children. Mrs W, a cousin of the mother, looked after the older three children but felt unable to cope with M as well, and he was placed in foster care. Mrs W obtained a residence order for the older three children. By the time of the final hearing for a care order for M, over one year later, Mrs W offered to have M as well. The special guardian wished the child to be adopted. The question arose as to whether the threshold criteria had been made out, a year later, so as to allow making a care order.

The House of Lords held that where, at the time the application is to be disposed of, there has been in place continuous protection of the child for some time, the relevant date with respect to which the court must be satisfied is the date at which the local authority initiated protection proceedings under the Act.

By the time the case reached the House of Lords M had been happily settled with Mrs W for several months. Therefore all parties agreed he should remain there.

Standard of proof

The question of future harm which the child is 'likely to suffer' should be judged 'on the balance of probabilities', as in *Re H and R (Child Sexual Abuse)* [1995]. However, the more serious the allegation the more urgent the evidence must be and it should be rigorously tested in cross examination. It is perfectly acceptable to base a finding of future risk of harm by looking at evidence of past events, even if those events did not occur within the current family grouping (*Re D* [1993]).

RE H AND R (Minors) (Sexual Abuse: Standard of Proof) [1995] 1 ALL ER 1 (HL)

There were allegations that the eldest of four daughters in a family had been sexually abused. Care proceedings were therefore brought in respect of three younger daughters on the ground that they were likely to suffer significant harm.

The trial judge held that he could not be sure to the requisite standard of proof that D's allegations of rape and sexual abuse were true and therefore the threshold criteria were not made out in respect of the younger children. However, the judge stated that he would be prepared to hold that there was a real possibility that her statement and her evidence was true.

The case was appealed to the House of Lords. All their Lordships agreed that the ordinary civil standard applies but they were divided on whether it should be a simple balance of probabilities test without any further gloss. Lord Nicholls gave the majority judgment, that when assessing probabilities the court should bear in mind that the more serious the allegation the less likely it is that the event occurred and, hence, the stronger should be the evidence before the court concludes that the allegation is established on the balance of probability. The balance of probability does not mean more likely than not but that there is a real possibility of significant harm having regard to the nature and gravity of the harm feared in the particular case.

The court should look at all the evidence and decide whether or not the child will suffer harm in the future if no order is made. It has been held that the words should not be construed restrictively and a CO should be granted if indicated by the evidence (*Re A (A Minor) (Care Proceedings)* [1993]).

Where it is unclear who the perpetrator of significant harm is

Where abuse has occurred and it is unclear which parent did it the child would be at risk of suffering significant harm if returned home and therefore the s 33 criteria are made out: *Re CB & JB* [1998] 2 FLR 211.

See also *Lancashire CC v B* [2000] 1 FLR 583 where it was not known if the harm was attributable to either parent or the nanny.

RE CB & JB [1998] 2 FLR 211

CB had suffered significant harm; however, it was not possible to establish who the perpetrator of the harm was. Both parents were possible abusers of CB. Their other child, JB, had not been injured. Prior to the court hearing the father had moved out of the family home.

Notwithstanding the fact that the father had moved out of the home the court held that the threshold in relation to JB was met, because abuse had occurred and even though it was not known which parent did it, both children would be at risk if returned home.

RE B & W [1999] 2 FLR 833; LANCASHIRE CC v B [2000] 1 FLR 583 (in the House of Lords)

A seven month old baby suffered serious injuries due to violent shaking. These injuries occurred either when she was being looked after by her parents, or by her child minder. The child minder also had a baby (B). B had not suffered any injury. The local authority brought care proceedings for both children based on the fact that the baby 'is suffering' significant harm and B was 'likely to suffer'.

The trial judge could not make a clear finding of fact as to who had caused these injuries and therefore felt compelled to hold that the threshold criteria were not met in respect of either child.

On appeal the Court of Appeal allowed the appeal in respect of the baby but dismissed it in respect of child B. The parents of the baby appealed. They argued that the threshold test could not be established where the court had not been able to satisfy itself that the harm suffered by the child was attributable to the care provided by the parents themselves.

The House of Lords dismissed the parents' appeal. In considering the statute their Lordships held that the term 'attributable' means a causal connection of some kind, not necessarily a strong connection, and it does not import any degree of responsibility or culpability. Where care of a child is shared between several adults and the child suffers significant harm that child must not be left at risk simply because the court cannot be sure which part of the care network is responsible.

Risk to a second child?

Where one child in the family has been harmed by an unknown perpetrator it would be highly unusual for the court not to find the threshold criteria made out for another child of the family: *Re K (Care: Threshold Criteria)* [2006] 2 FLR 868.

RE K (Care: Threshold Criteria) [2006] 2 FLR 868

The trial judge when considering whether the 'significant' harm threshold was satisfied so as to make a care order, took into account his local knowledge of the behaviour of parents in the area. The judge dismissed the child's non-attendance at school and witnessing of domestic violence, on the basis that if this were to establish significant harm the local authority would be seeking thousands of care orders.

The Court of Appeal held that the level of domestic violence here was so bad that the child either had, or was likely to, suffer significant harm. The court agreed that on its own the non-attendance was probably not enough, but when it was coupled with other factors such as the domestic violence it made it much more important.

Standard of parenting

When looking at the second part of the criteria, the harm being considered must arise from the care being given by the child's parent not amounting to what would be expected from a reasonable parent; that is, an objective test applies.

The parents' parenting skills need not be perfect. It is generally accepted by the courts that children are better brought up by their parents and therefore society must be willing to tolerate diverse standards of parenting: *Re B (Care: Threshold Criteria)* [2007] 1 FLR 2050.

RE B (Care: Threshold Criteria) [2007] 1 FLR 2050

The parents of two children both had severe learning difficulties. There were allegations of domestic violence and poor care of the children. However, Mr Justice Hedley when considering whether this was sufficient to establish the threshold criteria, held that society must be willing to tolerate very diverse standards of parenting, including the eccentric, the barely adequate and the inconsistent. Children will inevitably have very different experiences of parenting and very unequal consequences flowing from it

> as some children will experience disadvantage and harm, while others will flourish in atmospheres of loving security and emotional stability. These are the consequences of our fallible humanity and it is not the provenance of the state to spare children all the consequences of defective parenting.

However, when looking at the element of being 'beyond parental control', it need not be the parent's fault. It may be that, if the parent has tried to discipline the child but has failed, the child would then be beyond control and could be the subject of an application. The parent could ask the LA to make such an application, but it will be up to the authority to decide whether or not to do so.

How decisions on care orders will be reached

Section 31(2) minimum requirement

Then court will consider s 1 factors to decide if care order to be made

The effects of a care order

While a CO is in force in respect of the child, the LA will have parental responsibility for him (s 33).

It is important to remember that the court will not interfere with the way that the local authority will implement a CO. Since it is seen that Parliament intended that local authorities should be trusted to do as they see fit when dealing with children in their care, the court, having had the opportunity to study the authority's plan when deciding to make the order, should allow the authority to manage the situation and should not attach conditions to a CO (*Re T (A Minor) (Care Order: Conditions)* [1994]). One of the difficulties that will be faced by the courts will be the interface with the European Convention on Human Rights. It can be questioned whether the lack of supervision by the court on implementation of the care plan satisfies the requirement for judicial involvement (*R v W and B* [2001]).

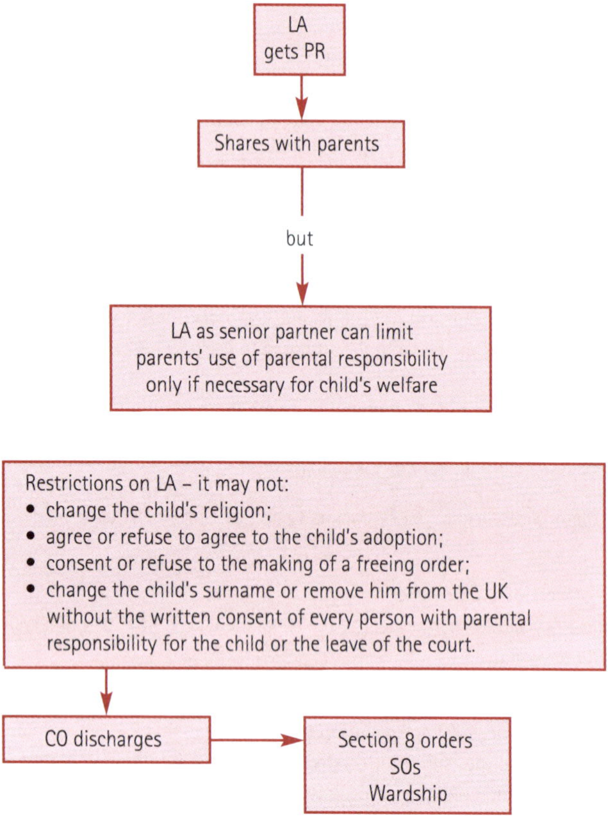

Parental contact with a child in care

Section 34 of the Act states that there is a statutory presumption that the authority must allow the child to have reasonable contact with certain groups of people after the granting of the order, and the authority is expected to present its proposals for contact to the court.

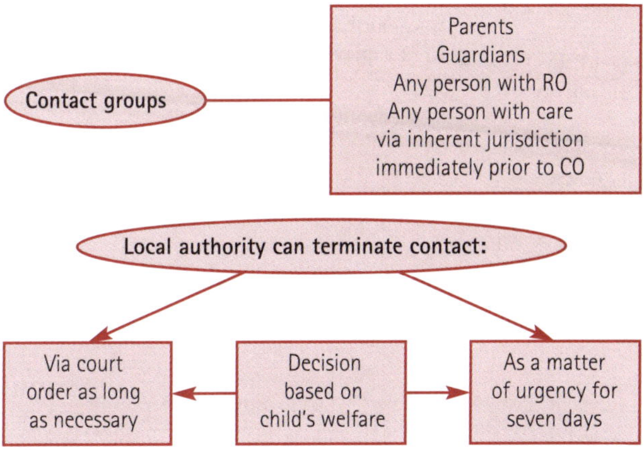

SUPERVISION ORDERS AND THEIR EFFECTS

An SO puts the child under the supervision of a local authority or a probation officer. The supervising body/officer does not acquire PR. Where the threshold criteria are made out, usually the court will have a choice in considering whether to make an SO or CO.

Schedule 3(4) states that an SO can require the child:

(a) to submit to a medical or psychiatric examination; and

(b) to submit to any such examination from time to time, as directed by the supervisor.

Schedule 4(4) states that no court may include such a requirement, unless satisfied that:

(a) where the child has sufficient understanding to make an informed decision, he consents to its inclusion; and

(b) satisfactory arrangements have been, or can be, made for the examination.

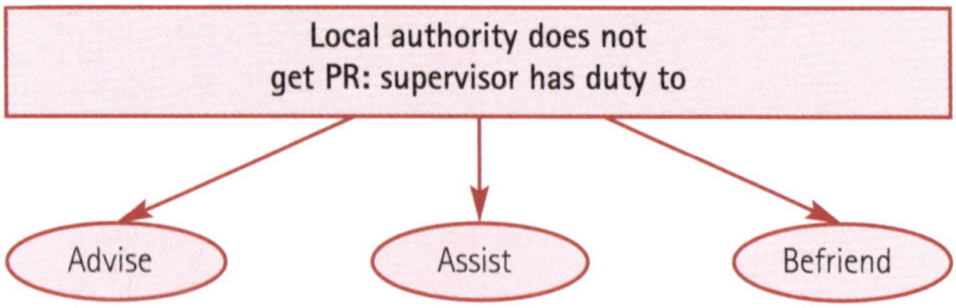

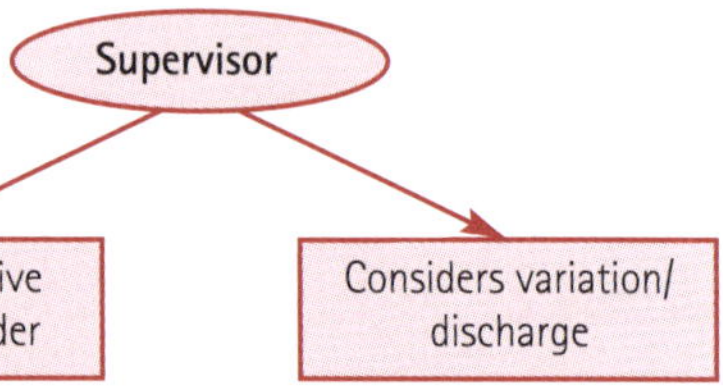

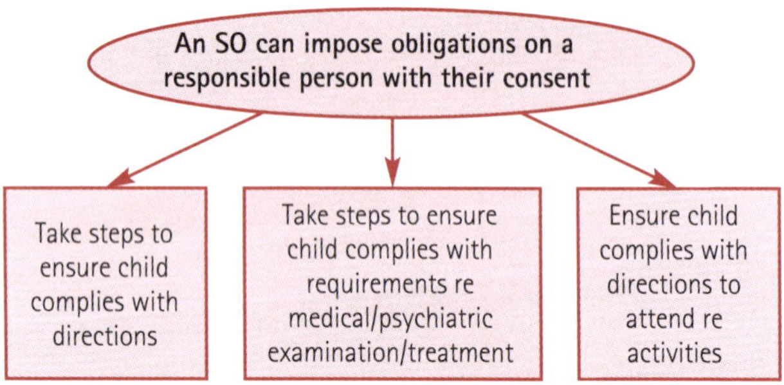

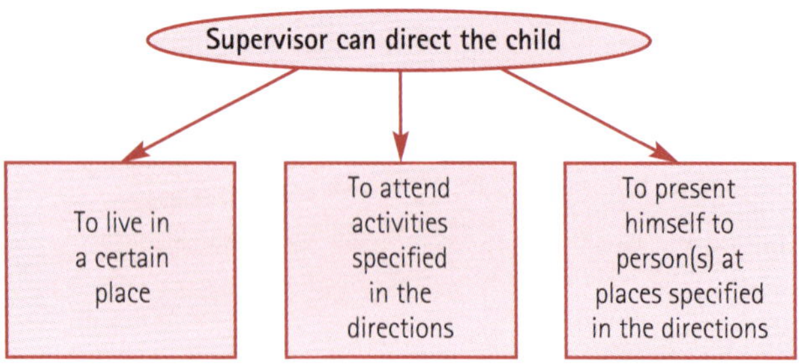

Duration: one year – possible extension up to three years

Schedule 3(3) states that a supervisor does not have power to give directions in respect of medical/psychiatric examination/treatment. This is a matter for the court.

Care order v supervision order – which one?

Re D (Care or Supervision Order) [2000] Fam Law 600
The court should ask itself whether:

(a) the stronger order is needed in order to protect the child;

(b) the risks could be met by a supervision order;

(c) there is a need for speed of action as afforded by a care order;

(d) there is a need for sharing parental responsibility with the LA;

(e) parental cooperation will only be obtained via a care order;

(f) the child's needs could be met by advising, assisting and befriending him;

(g) there have been any improvements observed during the current proceedings by objective observers.

Obviously, where the risks of significant harm are so high the child's welfare requires a care order: *Re C & B (Care Order: Future Harm)* [2001] 1 FLR 611.

Interim care orders and supervision orders – s 38

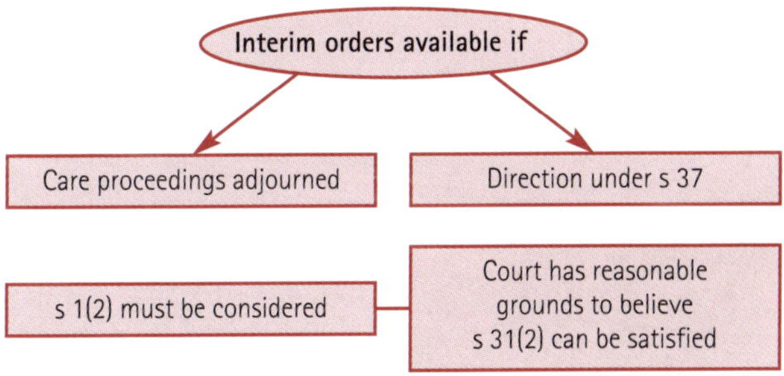

In most cases where the LA has applied for a CO or an SO, the court will be unable to reach a conclusion as to how finally to deal with a case and may need to make an interim order until further enquiries have been made and reports submitted for its consideration. The court can also make an interim order if, in the context of private law proceedings, it has requested an investigation of the child's situation by the LA, under s 37. This will normally occur when the court feels that the child is at risk of harm if they remain with their carers without suitable input from the LA.

The FLA 1996 has introduced s 38A into the CA 1989. This allows an exclusion requirement to be added to an interim CO if the court has reasonable cause to believe that:

- if a person is excluded from the child's home or prevented from entering it, the child will cease or cease to be likely to suffer significant harm;
- a person living in the house must be able and willing to care for the child and must consent to the requirement.

During the period of the interim CO, the court has the power to order assessments under s 38(6). While the section implies that these assessments are of the child, the House of Lords has indicated that assessment can be of the family if, by assessing, the court is then provided with all the relevant facts to make its decision. The fact that a family assessment may be expensive is irrelevant if it is necessary to the decision; the LA cannot plead poverty and hence fetter the court's discretion – *Re C (Interim Care Order: Residential Assessment)* [1997].

DISCHARGE OF A CARE ORDER

The court will decide the matter on the principles contained in s 1 of the Act.

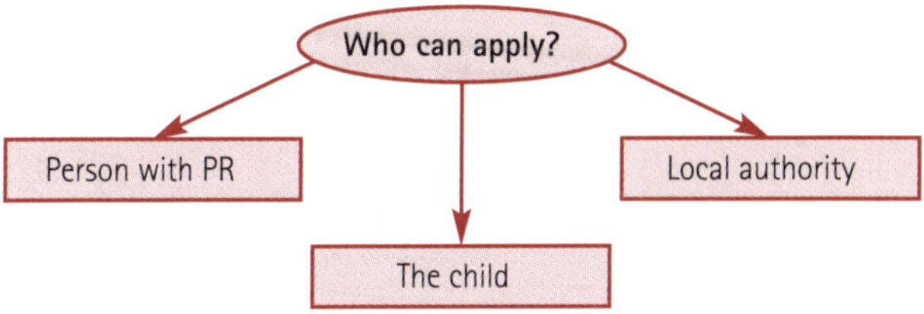

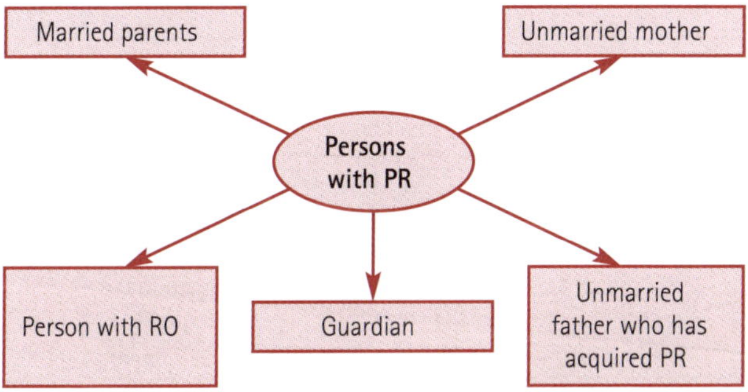

Others would need leave to apply for a RO. If granted, a RO would vest PR in the applicant and end the CO. If the applicant is the LA, the court may substitute an SO in place of the CO – there is no need to prove s 31(2) again. If the application is refused, no further applications may be made within six months without leave of the court.

APPOINTMENT OF A CHILDREN'S GUARDIAN

Section 41(1) of the Act states that, in care and supervision proceedings, a children's guardian (formerly called the guardian ad litem) must be appointed to represent the child unless they are not needed to safeguard the child's interests.

The children's guardian is an independent social worker; that is, he is not employed by the local authority involved in the proceedings.

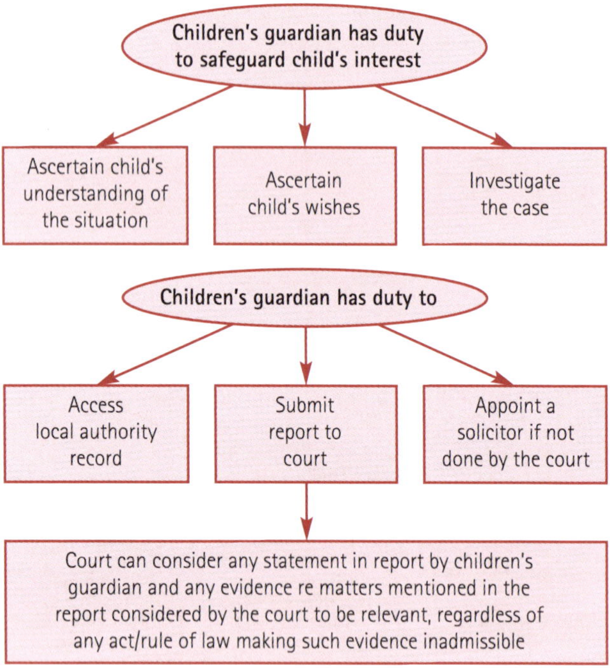

A solicitor may also be appointed by the children's guardian, unless one has already been appointed by the court. The children's guardian will give the solicitor instructions on the child's behalf unless the child has sufficient understanding to do so himself.

WARDSHIP AND INHERENT JURISDICTION

The wardship jurisdiction of the court is used to protect the interests of children where parental responsibility for the child rests with the court. If wardship is granted, then the child will often stay with the party that made the application, but that party will not be able to take any important decision in the child's life without the consent of the court, which can also give directions to safeguard the welfare of the child (*Re S* [1967]).

The inherent jurisdiction of the High Court is the use of the power of the Crown as *parens patriae*. This stems from the duty of the Crown to protect its subjects. The inherent jurisdiction is theoretically without limit, but, in practice, limits do apply. Where the inherent jurisdiction applies to children, it gives the court the ability to exceed the powers and overrule the decisions of parents and '*Gillick* competent' children (*Re W (A Minor) (Consent to Medical Treatment)* [1993]).

The inherent jurisdiction exists independently of wardship and can be used to protect the interests of a child who has not been made a ward. It is generally used to settle a specific issue, very often a medical matter, and as it deals with issues relating to PR, overlaps with certain s 8 orders under the CA 1989, for example specific issues orders.

A very clear example occurred in the case of *Re M (A Minor) (Medical Treatment)* [1999]. In this case, a 15½ year old girl refused to consent to a heart transplant, even though the doctors treating her considered that, without it, she would die.

The court was asked to overrule her refusal and allow the treatment to go ahead. The court followed the principle laid down in *Re W* and the treatment was carried out.

Wardship and the Children Act 1989

The CA 1989 has, as we have seen, introduced a flexible range of orders which are available to the court when dealing with 'family proceedings'. This has made the use of wardship much less likely than previously, and it will generally only be necessary in cases where the orders are unavailable or where speed is of the essence.

Private law matters

The CA 1989 has not placed any restriction on the use of wardship in private law matters. However, the wide range of powers in s 8 of the Act makes it more likely that the parties will use these orders rather than wardship.

There will be times when using wardship could be an advantage. If there is a leave requirement under the CA 1989, the use of wardship will avoid this. Also, if the element of continuing judicial control is thought to be necessary, then, again, wardship will be the better route to take (*Re G-U (A Minor) (Wardship)* [1984]).

Public law matters

Unlike private law matters, the area of public law in respect of wardship has been severely restricted by the CA 1989. Section 100(2) ensures that local authorities are no longer allowed to use wardship or the inherent jurisdiction to take children into care or make them subject to an SO.

However, there are situations where LAs are still able to use the inherent jurisdiction, albeit with the leave of the court (s 100(3)).

In order to grant leave, the court must be satisfied that:

- the result that the local authority wishes to achieve could not be achieved by the making of any other type of order which the local authority might be entitled to apply for under the statutory code; and
- there is reasonable cause to believe that, if the court's inherent jurisdiction is not exercised with respect to the child, he is likely to suffer significant harm.

Cases where such a cause has been found are where medical treatment was needed for a child who refused consent (*Re W (A Minor) (Medical Treatment: Court's Jurisdiction)* [1993]) and where publicity would be harmful to the child (*Essex CC v Mirror Group Newspapers* [1996]). Wardship is also useful where the child is over 17, since the LA cannot make an application for a CO/SO if the child is over this age and still below 18.

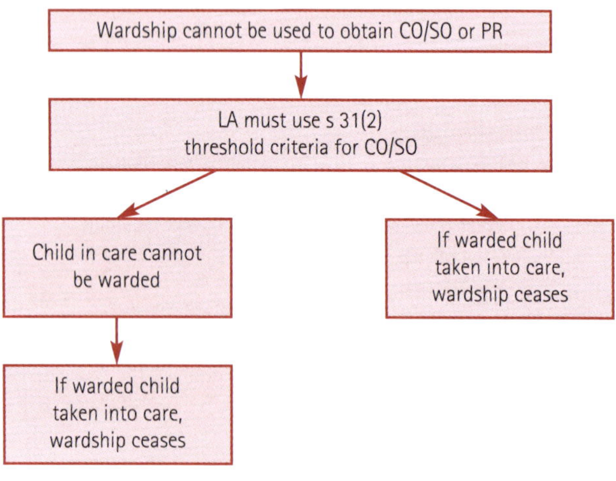

However, just because leave is granted, the inherent jurisdiction will not necessarily be exercised (*Essex CC v Mirror Group Newspapers* [1996]). It will still be necessary to show that significant harm is likely to occur; however, this usually causes no difficulty.

WARDSHIP APPLICATIONS

Wardship proceedings begin with originating summons in the Family Division at the High Court: the minor is warded when summons are issued.

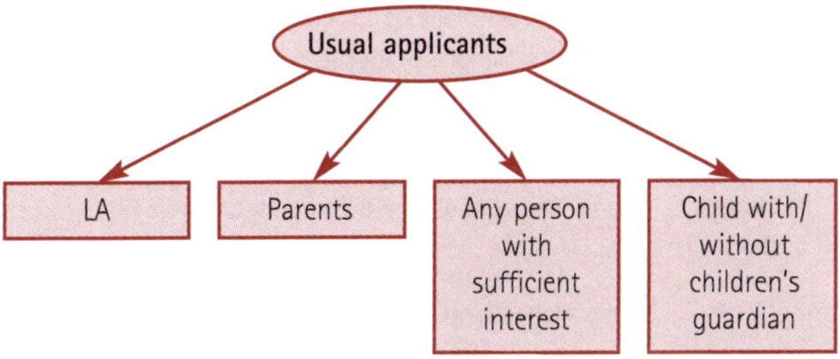

Publicity

In wardship proceedings, the court has the power to make an injunction prohibiting the publication of information which is considered harmful to the child. Any order made is binding on every person who is potentially subject to the order, even though they have not been joined as a party to the proceedings.

Although the publication of information relating to proceedings before any court sitting in private is not in itself a contempt, there are exceptions to this situation, including:

- proceedings which relate to the exercise of the inherent jurisdiction of the High Court in relation to minors;
- proceedings under the CA 1989; and
- any other proceedings which relate wholly or mainly to the maintenance or upbringing of a minor.

When deciding such matters, the court will *not* regard the welfare of the child as paramount, but it will regard the child's welfare as the most important consideration. The balance that the court will seek to achieve when reaching its decision will be between the welfare of the child and the public interest (*Re H (Minors) (Injunction: Public Interest)* [1993]).

ADOPTION

The process of adoption has changed by virtue of the Adoption and Children Act 2002.

s 46 ACA

(1) An adoption order is an order made by the court . . . giving parental responsibility for a child to the adopters or adopter.

(2) The adoption order operates to extinguish

(a) The parental responsibility which any person other than the adopter . . . has for the adopted child immediately before the making of the order . . .

An adoption order brings a legal adoption into being and ends a natural parent's parental responsibility, vesting it in the adoptive parents (s 67).

s 67 ACA

(1) An adopted person is to be treated in law as if born as the child of the adopter . . .

and

(3) . . . not being the child of any other person.

Thus an adoption order 'severs, irrevocably and for all time, the legal relationship between a child and her family of birth. It creates, irrevocably and for all time . . . a new legal relationship, not only between the child and her adoptive parents, but between the child and each of her adoptive parents families' per Baroness Hale in *Re P* [2008] UKHL 36.

It also ends any parental responsibility that any other person may have had for the child and brings to an end any order made under the CA 1989. However, such proceedings fall within the definition of 'family proceedings' and, as such, the court will be able to make use of s 8 orders in the proceedings, should they consider them necessary. This is most likely in the case of a step-parent seeking to adopt a stepchild.

Welfare of the child

When dealing with an application for an adoption order the child's welfare is the court's paramount concern, and the court will have a statutory checklist to consider. Whilst this checklist is similar to that in the CA 1989, it has some differences. The court will need to consider:

The Welfare Principle

Section 1 ACA: Considerations applying to the exercise of powers

(1) This section applies whenever a court or adoption agency is coming to a decision relating to the adoption of a child.

(2) The paramount consideration of the court or adoption agency must be the child's welfare, *throughout his life* [emphasis added].

(3) The court or adoption agency must at all times bear in mind that, in general, any delay in coming to the decision is likely to prejudice the child's welfare.

(4) The court or adoption agency must have regard to the following matters (among others)–
- (a) the child's ascertainable wishes and feelings regarding the decision (considered in the light of the child's age and understanding),
- (b) the child's particular needs,
- (c) the likely effect on the child (throughout his life) of having ceased to be a member of the original family and become an adopted person,
- (d) the child's age, sex, background and any of the child's characteristics which the court or agency considers relevant,
- (e) any harm (within the meaning of the Children Act 1989 (c. 41)) which the child has suffered or is at risk of suffering,
- (f) the relationship which the child has with relatives, and with any other person in relation to whom the court or agency considers the relationship to be relevant, including–
  - (i) the likelihood of any such relationship continuing and the value to the child of its doing so,

(ii) the ability and willingness of any of the child's relatives, or of any such person, to provide the child with a secure environment in which the child can develop, and otherwise to meet the child's needs,

(iii) the wishes and feelings of any of the child's relatives, or of any such person, regarding the child.

(5) In placing the child for adoption, the adoption agency must give due consideration to the child's religious persuasion, racial origin and cultural and linguistic background.

(6) The court or adoption agency must always consider the whole range of powers available to it in the child's case (whether under this Act or the Children Act 1989); and the court must not make any order under this Act unless it considers that making the order would be better for the child than not doing so.

Note that the child's interest is paramount. Although the relationship with the birth parents is clearly taken into account, there is no requirement to give separate consideration to the rights of the birth parents. However, there is a strong argument that Article 8 of the ECHR demands that their rights should be considered.

Who can adopt?

If the applicant is the step-parent of the child, or the partner of the parent, then s 52 provides that they can apply to adopt singly, and this will not affect the status of the parent in question (see figure opposite).

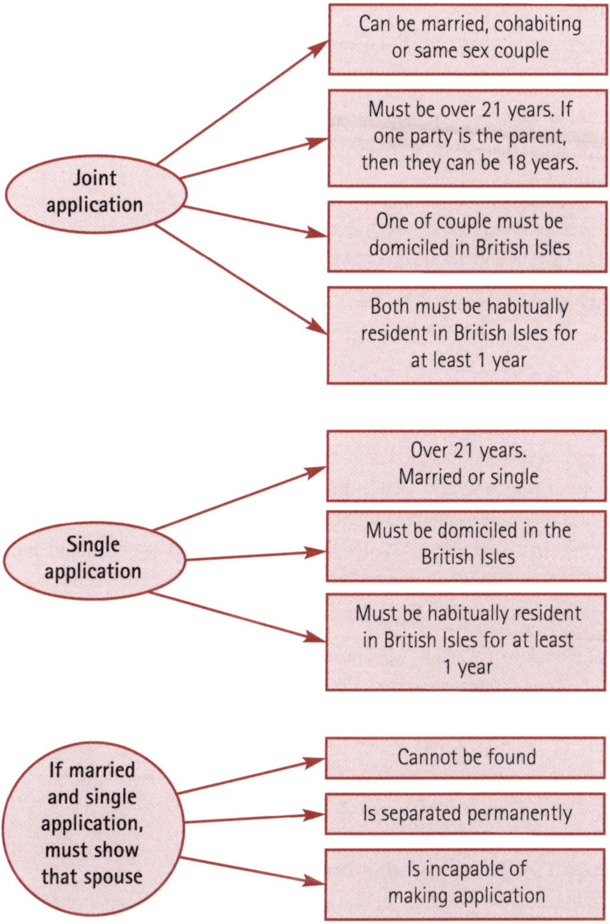

Who can be adopted (s 42 and s 47)

- Child must be less than 18 years old at date of application and is not, and has not been, married.
- Child must have lived with applicants for requisite time.

- If applicants or local authority foster parent and placement was not for purposes of adoption, the child must have lived with applicants for at least one year.
- Where applicant is parent, or child has been placed with applicants by an adoption agency or the High Court, the child must have lived with applicants for 10 weeks.
- For all other applicants, the child must have lived with applicants (or if a couple, with one or both of them) for not less than 3 years in preceding 5 years.
- Where the applicant is the partner of the child's parent, the child must have lived with applicant for 6 months.

Placement for adoption

Placement for adoption will normally arise via the intervention of an adoption agency. However, as has been seen, this is not the only situation when an adoption order will be sought. Hence the Adoption and Children Act 2002 enables partners of a child's parent to apply; as can local authority foster parents where the child was placed for the purposes of fostering (and not adoption) and any other person with whom the child has lived for the requisite period (although this is likely to be aimed at relatives).

Local authority placement will arise via the application of s 19 or s 21 and can only be done if the authority is of the opinion that the child ought to be placed for adoption (s 18). It should be noted that local authorities have a discretionary power to impose conditions on who they deem suitable to be an adoptive parent, for example in relation to the maximum age of the adopters and their lifestyle (smoking, weight and other health issues).

Section 19 – placement with parental consent

Once the child has reached the age of 6 weeks, the parents can give consent to placement for adoption, and advance consent to the adoption order. Consent is defined as made 'unconditionally and with full understanding of what is involved' (s 52) but the parent(s) do not need to know the identity of the adopters.

Subject to this, the adoption process cannot move forward unless (a) there is parental consent or (b) the court has ordered that parental consent can be dispensed with in accordance with s 52(1) on the grounds that:

(a) The parent . . . cannot be found or in incapable of giving consent.

(b) The welfare of the child *requires* the consent be dispensed with [Emphasis added].

Again, and in contrast to the position under the AA 1976 which gave more scope for parental views to be taken into account, there is a simple welfare test which appears to focus exclusively on the child.

Re P (Children) (Placement Orders: Parental Consent) [2008] (CA)

Children subject to care orders and LA then applied for placement orders (see below) to enable search for potential adoptive as well as foster parents, it being accepted that children could not be cared for by either natural parent or another family member. Mother objected to placement orders on basis they would jeopardise her contact with the children. Judge dispensed with parental consent to the placement orders, concluding that the need for the LA to have the widest possible pool of carers available to it outweighed the risk that contact would be lost. Mother appealed.

Held: Judge had applied the proper test for dispensing with parental agreement in the making of a placement order. The issue depended on the meaning of 'welfare' in s 52(1)(b). The answer was to be found in s 1(2) which required the court to treat the child's welfare *throughout his life* as its paramount consideration. In summary, the best guidance the court could give was to advise judges to apply the statutory language with care to the facts of the particular case. The European Convention on Human Rights 1950 art. 8 was plainly engaged, and any interference had to be proportionate to the aim of protecting the welfare of the child. The word 'requires' in s 52(1)(b) had the connotation of the imperative, and meant that which was required rather than that which was merely optional, reasonable or desirable. Moreover, it had to be shown that the child's welfare required adoption as opposed to something short of adoption.

However, case-law from the ECtHR suggests that the birth parents have independent rights which should be taken into account.

A parent is defined as a parent with parental responsibility: s 52(6). The consent of an unmarried father without PR is therefore not required. The mother can give unilateral consent for the child's adoption where the identity of the father is unknown or such information is not forthcoming: *Re L (Adoption: Contacting Natural Father)* [2007].

Section 21 – placement by placement order

A placement order is one that authorises the local authority to place the child with a view to adoption. The ACA 2002 sets out various criteria that set the boundaries upon the use of this order:

- the child must be subject to a care order; or
- the court think the criteria for making a care order would be met; or
- the child has no parent or guardian; or
- the parent(s) have consented to the order; or
- the court feels that this consent should be dispensed with.

Where the child is subject to a care order, and the parent(s) give consent as required by s 19, the local authority may, but does not have to, apply for a placement order. It is likely to be the case that they will always apply for the placement order, but if consent is not forthcoming, a placement order will have to be sought.

Dispensing with consent

Unlike the preceding legislation, there are only two grounds upon which parental consent to the placement for adoption can be dispensed with. Section 52 deals with this:

- the court must be satisfied that the parent or guardian cannot be found; or
- the court must be satisfied that the welfare of the child requires that consent be dispensed with.

Making the adoption order

When the application for the adoption order is made, the court has to be satisfied that the adopters meet the legal requirements in terms of age, domicile and habitual residence, and also that the child has lived with them for the requisite time. They must also be satisfied that it is in the child's welfare to be adopted, using the welfare checklist highlighted earlier. The court must ensure that consent has been given for the making of the adoption order, or that this consent can be dispensed with, which is on the same grounds as dispensing with consent to the making of a placement order.

Revoking the adoption order

Once made an adoption order cannot be revoked or appealed against, unless it was made *ultra vires* (see *Re K* [1997]). However, there is nothing to stop an adopted child being adopted by someone else at a later stage. All the above requirements would need to be satisfied.

You should now be confident that you would be able to tick all of the boxes on the checklist at the beginning of this chapter. To check your knowledge of Children II why not visit the companion website and take the Multiple Choice Question test. Check your understanding of the terms and vocabulary used in this chapter with the flashcard glossary.

7

Putting it into practice ...

.hat you've mastered the basics, you will want to put it all into practice. The Routledge Questions and Answers series provides an ideal opportunity for you to apply your understanding and knowledge of the law and to hone your essay-writing technique.

We've included one exam-style essay question, which replicates the type of question posed in the Routledge Questions and Answers series to give you some essential exam practice. The Q&A includes an answer plan and a fully worked model answer to help you recognise what examiners might look for in your answer.

QUESTION 1

Jane, an Englishwoman, went to Ruritania to work, and there she met and married Fred, a Ruritanian man with whom she had fallen in love. He told her that although the law of his country allowed him to take more than one wife, he felt that she was so special he would never do so. After a few months Jane tired of his adoring, but boring, company and decided to return home. She soon forgot about Fred and began to form a relationship with Tarzan, who had been briefly married to Jane's mother. Jane's mother had died two years previously and shortly after meeting, Jane and Tarzan married. However, after the ceremony Jane could not bring herself to have sexual intercourse with Tarzan, as she is tormented by the thought of his relationship with her mother.

- Advise Jane on the validity of her marriages.

Answer Plan

Begin by examining the validity of the marriage to Fred:

- consider if both parties had capacity;
- this depends on where they were domiciled at the time of marriage;
- the effect of the polygamous, or potentially polygamous, nature of the marriage.

Then consider the validity of the marriage to Tarzan:

- consider capacity;
- problem of prohibited degrees;
- problem if Jane is already validly married to Fred.

Consider also the possibility that the marriage is voidable:

- non-consummation (incapacity or wilful refusal?)

ANSWER

In advising Jane on the validity of her marriages, it will be necessary to examine the first marriage to Fred, which took place in Ruritania. For this marriage to be valid, both parties must have had capacity to marry and the relevant formalities must have been complied with.

Turning to the issue of capacity, English case law has determined this by reference to two different tests. Cases such as *In the Will of Swan* [1871] have judged the validity of the marriage by examining whether the parties had capacity to marry by reference to the law of the 'intended matrimonial home'. This has the advantage of requiring only one jurisdiction to be examined, and treats marriage on a par with other contracts by examining its validity according to the jurisdiction the marriage has the closest connection to. It is the test most likely to render a marriage valid. However, the intended matrimonial home test is vague and uncertain, and problems may be encountered if the parties do not go on to set up a matrimonial home in the jurisdiction.

The second test requires the parties to have capacity by reference to the law of their respective domiciles before they married. This is the test favoured by the Law Commission as being more certain, and it viewed testing the validity of marriage by reference to something existing at the time of the marriage preferable to testing the validity by reference to something that can only really be established after the marriage takes place. Applying this test in the present case it must be established that each party to the marriage had capacity to marry according to the law of their ante-nuptial domicile, *Sottomayer v de Barros (No 1)* [1877].

Fred was domiciled in Ruritania. Ruritania was clearly his permanent home: *Whicker v Hume* [1858]. Thus Fred would seem to have capacity to marry Jane, although it is arguable whether Jane had capacity to marry Fred. She begins with an English domicile. However, when she goes to Ruritania to work, she may have obtained a Ruritanian domicile of choice. To establish this it would be necessary for her to have made Ruritania her permanent home, that is, established a physical presence of a lasting nature, with an intention to make it her permanent home. This intention must be positive and demonstrate a fixed and settled intention to remain; mere indifference on Jane's part would not suffice (*Winans v AG* [1910]). In going to Ruritania to work, Jane's intentions are not clear. If she intended this as a temporary or transient measure then there is insufficient determination to acquire a domicile of choice. However, if on meeting Fred, Jane decides that she should settle in Ruritania then she may have acquired a Ruritanian domicile of choice.

If Jane is domiciled in Ruritania at the time of her marriage to Fred then she will also have capacity to marry, notwithstanding the potentially polygamous nature of the marriage, as Ruritanian law allows polygamy. It is assumed that the requisite formalities of Ruritanian law, which is the *lex loci*, have been complied with, and so the marriage will be valid: *Herbert v Herbert* [1819].

There is, however, a strong possibility that Jane was still domiciled in England at the time of her marriage to Fred, in which case her capacity must be judged according to English law. Lord Penzance in *Hyde v Hyde* [1866] defined marriage as 'the voluntary union of a man and a woman for life to the exclusion of all others' and this definition has formed the basis of the English law rules on capacity. To be able to contract a valid marriage, an English domiciliary must be over 16 (which it is assumed Jane and Fred are); not within the prohibited degrees of relationship (which again appears to cause no difficulty here); not already married; and the marriage must not be polygamous. This is the aspect of the marriage that requires greater examination.

The Matrimonial Causes Act 1973 s 11(d) provides that a marriage that is polygamous is void. This means that the marriage is treated as a complete nullity, and there is no need to obtain a nullity decree unless financial provision is to be sought under s 23 or 24 of the Act. In the instant case the marriage is not actually polygamous, but it has the potential, given Fred's domicile, to become polygamous. In *Hussain v Hussain* [1982] a marriage between a man and a woman in Pakistan which permitted polygamy was nevertheless held to be valid, as the woman had the Pakistani domicile and could not take a second husband, and the man had an English domicile and could not take a second wife, thereby rendering the marriage monogamous. This would not apply to the marriage between Jane and Fred, as the roles are reversed and Fred could still, in theory, take another spouse. Thus the marriage between Jane and Fred, whilst not actually polygamous, is potentially so. Until the provisions of the Private

International Law (Miscellaneous Provisions) Act 1995 (PIL (MP) A) came into force in 1996, the MCA 1973 s 11(d) had the effect of making a potentially polygamous marriage by an English domiciliary void. This somewhat discriminatory rule was the subject of criticism by the Law Commission in their report on polygamous marriages, which thought that the rule as relating to potentially polygamous marriages was harsh. Accordingly the PIL (MP) A 1995 s 5 amended s 11(d) to make marriages that were only potentially polygamous valid. The Act has retrospective effect, s 6(1), but it does not retrospectively validate a potentially polygamous marriage if a party to that marriage has gone on to celebrate a later valid marriage, s 6(2).

In Jane and Fred's case, we are not told when their marriage took place. If it took place after the provisions of the PIL (MP) A 1995 were in force, then it is valid. If it took place before this date, then it may still be valid, provided neither party has gone on to celebrate a subsequent valid marriage.

It therefore seems that if Jane was domiciled in England, the first marriage's status will depend upon when it took place and the status of any second marriage, whereas if she were domiciled in Ruritania it would be valid. English law will not refuse to recognise valid polygamous marriages for public policy reasons: *Mohammed v Knott* [1969]. The second marriage will be valid if both parties have capacity by the law of their ante-nuptial domiciles and have complied with the requisite formalities. Both Tarzan and Jane are domiciled in England at the time of the marriage and are male and female and above the age of 16. There is, however, a potential problem given that for a short while Tarzan was married to Jane's mother. There would be an absolute prohibition on Jane marrying Tarzan if he were her natural or adoptive father; likewise if she had at any stage been a child of the family whilst Tarzan was married to her mother: Marriage Act 1949 Sched 1. However, if Jane had never been treated by Tarzan as a child of the family and Tarzan's relationship with Jane's mother had occurred when Jane was no longer living at home, then provided that Tarzan and Jane are both over 21 they will be able to marry: Marriage (Prohibited Degrees) Act 1986. However, an additional problem may be encountered if the first marriage to Fred was valid. English law requires both parties to be single, and if one or more of them is already married then the subsequent marriage is a nullity: MCA 1973 s 11(b). If the marriage to Fred was valid then the marriage to Tarzan will be void. However, if the marriages to Fred and Tarzan took place before the provisions of the PIL (MP) A 1995 came into force then the marriage to Fred is void as potentially polygamous, and the marriage to Tarzan will be valid. This is because the retrospective nature of the provisions does not operate if there has been a second valid marriage according to the law at the time it was celebrated.

There are possible grounds for arguing that the marriage between Jane and Tarzan is voidable for one of the reasons in the MCA s 12. It does not seem that the marriage has been consummated. Jane's attitude has ensured that there has been no complete and regular intercourse (*D v A* [1845]) once the marriage has taken place. Premarital intercourse does not suffice for consummation. It is then necessary to consider whether this is due to incapacity to consummate or wilful refusal.

Either party can petition on the basis that there is some physical or psychological reason preventing consummation (*D v D* [1982]). Here it would seem that Jane has psychological problems that are preventing intercourse. In order for the decree to be granted these reasons must exist at the date of the petition and the date of the hearing (*Napier v Napier* [1915]), but there must also be no practical possibility of intercourse (*S v S* [1962]). In the instant case it is not clear what, if anything at all, can be done to help Jane; neither is it apparent that she wishes to be helped to overcome the problem. If it is felt that there is a possibility of intercourse should Jane accept help which would not expose her to too great a risk, then Jane's refusal to seek such assistance may amount to a wilful refusal to consummate. This would be a settled and definite decision without just cause (*Horton v Horton* [1947]), and would give Tarzan the opportunity to petition for nullity.

A voidable marriage is valid unless and until it is dissolved by way of nullity decree (*De Renville v De Renville* [1948]), unlike the void marriage. Therefore, Jane should seek a nullity decree in respect of her marriage to Tarzan.

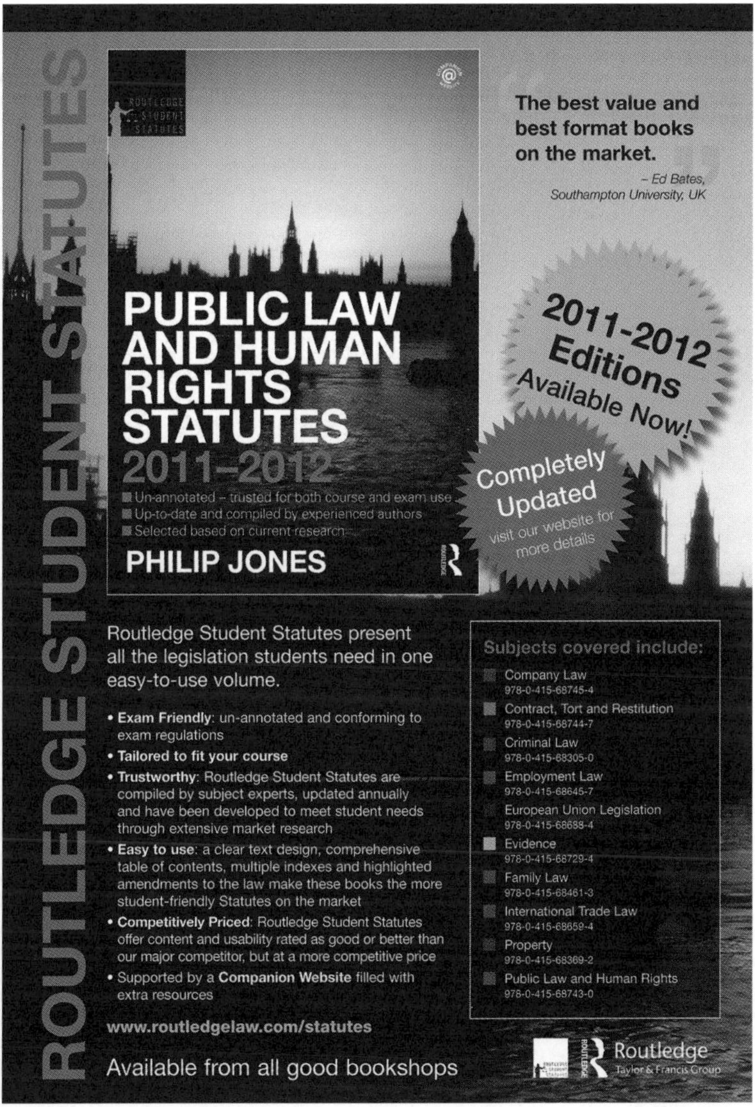
ROUTLEDGE STUDENT STATUTES
ROUTLEDGE STUDENT STATUTES
PUBLIC LAW AND HUMAN RIGHTS STATUTES
2011–2012
Un-annotated – trusted for both course and exam use
Up-to-date and compiled by experienced authors
Selected based on current research
PHILIP JONES
The best value and best format books on the market.
– Ed Bates, Southampton University, UK
2011-2012 Editions Available Now!
Completely Updated
visit our website for more details
Routledge Student Statutes present all the legislation students need in one easy-to-use volume.
• Exam Friendly: un-annotated and conforming to exam regulations
• Tailored to fit your course
• Trustworthy: Routledge Student Statutes are compiled by subject experts, updated annually and have been developed to meet student needs through extensive market research
• Easy to use: a clear text design, comprehensive table of contents, multiple indexes and highlighted amendments to the law make these books the more student-friendly Statutes on the market
• Competitively Priced: Routledge Student Statutes offer content and usability rated as good or better than our major competitor, but at a more competitive price
• Supported by a Companion Website filled with extra resources
Subjects covered include:
Company Law 978-0-415-68745-4
Contract, Tort and Restitution 978-0-415-68744-7
Criminal Law 978-0-415-68305-0
Employment Law 978-0-415-68645-7
European Union Legislation 978-0-415-68688-4
Evidence 978-0-415-68729-4
Family Law 978-0-415-68461-3
International Trade Law 978-0-415-68659-4
Property 978-0-415-68369-2
Public Law and Human Rights 978-0-415-68743-0
www.routledgelaw.com/statutes
Available from all good bookshops
Routledge
Taylor & Francis Group